P9-CAO-839

ADVANCE PRAISE FOR
The Prayer Wheel

A brilliant rediscovery. *The Prayer Wheel* reveals how important prayer has been in all of history, and how many levels of understanding it always offers. This is an excellent example of the endless fruitfulness of healthy religion."

—Richard Rohr, author of *Falling Upward*

"This bold recovery of a long-forgotten path to prayer, expertly situated in its historical context and made accessible for modern-day believers, makes for absolutely fascinating reading—for the devout and doubtful alike."

—James Martin, SJ, author of *Jesus: A Pilgrimage*

"Reading this book for the first time, I felt the way I felt when someone first told me about labyrinths—I was encountering something that could carry me both back into the depths of an ancient practice, and forward to God."

—Lauren F. Winner, author of *Girl Meets God* and *Still*

"I am always looking for ways to engage in prayer more deeply. Beautifully written and biblically grounded, this book offers readers a fresh yet ancient way of drawing close to God. Because of its simplicity and depth, I am sure I will enjoy using it for years to come."

—Ann Spangler, author of *Praying the Names of God*

"This remarkable book isn't just a guide to a long-lost medieval prayer wheel, but an introduction to a deeper, more fulfilling way of communicating with God."

—Ian Morgan Cron, author of *The Road Back to You: An Enneagram Journey to Self-Discovery*

"Like Benedict in his own day, we are searching for new ways to connect ancient wisdom with daily life in a rapidly changing world. In this midst of this transition, Dodd, Riess, and Van Biema offer a contemporary introduction to an ancient way of prayer. This prayer wheel may be just the tool to unlock the door to the home you always knew you needed."

—Jonathan Wilson-Hartgrove, coauthor of *Common Prayer: A Liturgy for Ordinary Radicals*

"If Indiana Jones were interested in medieval Christian spirituality, he'd have loved *The Prayer Wheel*! Dodd, Riess, and Van Biema unlock the mystery of an ancient Christian path to prayer, then help modern readers apply it for a meaningful spiritual journey."

—Adam Hamilton, author of *Unafraid: Living with Courage and Hope in Uncertain Times,* and *Creed: What Christians Believe and Why*

"It's rare these days to be truly surprised by something, especially something old. Yet that was my experience of reading and engaging with *The Prayer Wheel*. For those of us who long to connect to our forebears in faith and who find too much of the modern world annoying and shallow, this book is a beautiful, reflective prayer aid."

—Tony Jones, author of *The Sacred Way: Spiritual Practices for Everyday Life*

"*The Prayer Wheel* opens a door into the prayer life of Christians who lived nearly a thousand years ago. Through meditation on brief but rich phrases of Scripture, we deepen and strengthen our faith."

—Frederica Mathewes-Green, author of *The Jesus Prayer* and *Facing East*

"How is it possible in our high-tech age that one of the most interesting new developments I've come across is a piece of technology that dates back to the Middle Ages? Whether you're a prayer veteran or novice spiritual seeker, *The Prayer Wheel* offers a way to approach our conversations with God that is both ancient and new."

—Bill McGarvey, former editor in chief of Busted Halo

"Our medieval Christian ancestors may not have understood growth economics, but they knew the value of praying in circles . . . with a prayer wheel, with a rosary, with the weekly and yearly cycles of the Divine Office. Here is all we have forgotten of the past, and all we might hope for the future, inscribed in a simple diagram—a cure for the linear, dead-end way of thinking that has brought our world to a precipice."

—Clark Strand, author of *Waking Up to the Dark: Ancient Wisdom for a Sleepless Age*

The
PRAYER WHEEL

The
PRAYER WHEEL

*A Daily Guide to Renewing Your Faith
with a Rediscovered Spiritual Practice*

Patton Dodd, Jana Riess, AND David Van Biema

Foreword by James Martin, SJ

CONVERGENT BOOKS
NEW YORK

Copyright © 2018 by Patton Dodd, Jana Riess, and David Van Biema

All rights reserved.
Published in the United States by Convergent Books, an imprint of the
Crown Publishing Group, a division of Penguin Random House LLC,
New York.
crownpublishing.com

CONVERGENT BOOKS is a registered trademark and its C colophon
is a trademark of Penguin Random House LLC.

Scripture quotations are from New Revised Standard Version Bible, copyright
© 1989 National Council of the Churches of Christ in the United States of
America. Used by permission. All rights reserved.

Library of Congress Cataloging-in-Publication Data is available upon request.

ISBN 978-1-5247-6031-1
Ebook ISBN 978-1-5247-6032-8

PRINTED IN THE UNITED STATES OF AMERICA

Prayer Wheel illustrations: Darrel Frost. Used by permission.
Cover design: Jessie Sayward Bright
*Cover illustration and Latin counterpart on page 3: Pater noster diagram, The
Liesborn Gospels: Gospel Book, Liesborn Abbey, Westphalia/Les Enluminures. Used
by permission.*

10 9 8 7 6 5 4 3 2 1

First Edition

We dedicate this book to all those who pray—or would like to try.

Each of us also would like to make a personal dedication:

Patton: To Mom

Jana: To Phyllis Tickle

David: To Allison Adato and Julian Van Biema

Stand at the crossroads, and look,
and ask for the ancient paths,
where the good way lies; and walk in it,
and find rest for your souls.

JEREMIAH 6:16

CONTENTS

PART 3
Praying the Scriptures with the Wheel
149

PART 4
The Bands of the Wheel
181

A New, Old Way to Pray

Sometimes returning to ancient sources is exactly what we need to renew our spiritual lives.

I felt the promise of something new when my friend David Van Biema first showed me a rough sketch of the Liesborn Prayer Wheel. This medieval invitation to prayer draws on the Our Father and other biblical texts that I had seen many times before, yet it points to a way of praying that was quite new to me.

The Our Father (a.k.a. the Lord's Prayer) is obviously an old prayer, one taught by Jesus to his disciples when they asked him for a way to pray. For some people, sadly, the prayer can seem too old. Thanks to the most popular English translation, it comes wrapped in archaic words and phrases—*hallowed, trespasses, thys,* and *thines*—that don't mirror our everyday way of speaking. As a result, some may feel that the prayer distances them from God, rather than drawing them closer.

But the Our Father stands at the heart of Christian tradition for good reasons. Of course the best reason is that it's the prayer that Jesus himself recommended. But there's something else: part of the good news (which is the meaning of the word "Gospel") that Jesus brought to the world is contained in the prayer—the message that God is love, that God loves us, and that all of us can live in that love. Much of what we are invited to understand about Jesus's vision for the world is highlighted in the Our Father: worship, acceptance, gratitude, trust, peace. The prayer shows us ways of entering into how the Gospel "works," if we let it.

Whoever—priest, brother, sister, layperson—created the Prayer Wheel nearly 1,000 years ago must have known a great deal about the spiritual life. They created an ingeniously compact design that opens up countless insights, connections, and prayer possibilities. The individual elements of the wheel may be familiar to you—the Our Father, the Gifts of the Holy Spirit, the Beatitudes, and key events from the Life of Christ. Yet along the paths of the wheel, these elements are combined in new ways, revealing connections that you might never have noticed.

For me, the Prayer Wheel offered an unfamiliar, and therefore fresh, look at words and ideas I've known my whole life. The wheel doesn't just offer a new way to *think about* these concepts; it invites us into a new way to *pray with* them, to explore them inwardly, and to make new discoveries as we learn to more fully orient our lives toward God and respond to God's grace.

You can pray or meditate your way along any circle, path, or combination of words you choose. But the authors have done us a service in writing a guide to its most powerful suggestion: breaking the Our Father and the other texts into seven elements (as St. Augustine and other early Church teachers did), then grouping those elements together into new prayer paths. In this way, they present a new way of praying that I hope you'll come to cherish, and return to often.

My own suggestion is to follow the prayer practices that the authors have laid out. Then experiment. There is no one "right" way to pray the wheel, just as there's no "right" way to pray. Personalize your prayer journey. Listen to where the Holy Spirit might be guiding you. I'll bet that the anonymous creator of the Prayer Wheel would agree on this: whatever path draws you closer to God is the right prayer path for you.

If you, like me, are struggling in these noisy times, a new practice of prayer comes at the perfect moment. Looking to wisdom from the past can help us live more contemplatively in the present. The Prayer Wheel may have returned to us just in time.

James Martin, SJ, is a Jesuit priest, editor at large of *America* magazine, and the *New York Times* bestselling author of many books, including *Jesus: A Pilgrimage* and *The Jesuit Guide to (Almost) Everything.*

The
PRAYER WHEEL

Discovering the Prayer Wheel

Eliza* works as a research associate at a start-up. She attends church nearby, where she generally enjoys the teaching and the music, and has good friends. If asked, Eliza would say she's growing in her faith. But like so many, she might also admit that she struggles with prayer.

It used to be simple. As a child, and even through college, she prayed the way her parents taught her. But lately, she seems to have lost her voice. Should she pray spontaneously, just saying what's on her mind? Stick with the written prayers of the Church? Sit in silence? She's tried several approaches, some of which at least raised a spark. But nothing keeps her coming back.

Yet doing nothing would feel like abandoning her soul. What she wishes for is a prayer practice that's personal, rich, and rooted. Something that is based deep in the faith but that also grows with her.

Recently, a teaching pastor at Eliza's church gave her a copy of an intriguing diagram that fit on a single sheet of paper. He called it a "prayer wheel," and said it was a thousand-year-old aid to prayer. At first, it seemed mysterious—like a message from Middle Earth, or an ancient board game. But in this board game, she soon realized, every move was a prayer. The wheel was packed with big ideas,

* Eliza is a composite of several people who already use the Prayer Wheel.

but using it wasn't hard to learn. And the more she has used it, the deeper she feels drawn into her faith and an ongoing conversation with God.

The wheel is made up of concentric bands, like a target. Curving outside the outermost band is the sentence: "The order of the diagram written here teaches the return home." Each of the other bands contains a key Christian text divided into seven phrases. The phrases align themselves in seven spokes that form paths from the wheel's outer edges to the word "God," at the center.

Every day, Eliza takes a different path from rim to center. Each phrase is a stepping-stone on that day's prayer experience. Pausing at each, she lets the meanings and connotations of the path so far seep in.

Phrase by phrase, path by path, prayer is coming alive for Eliza in new ways. She is on a journey that feels new and refreshing—personal, yet rooted in sacred texts and in a praying tradition she has never encountered until now, tested by generations of spiritual pilgrims before her.

For Eliza, as it was for them, the destination is always home, whose name is God.

The Holy Book with the Extra Page

If you wonder why you've never heard of this diagram before, it's probably because until very recently, most of the world had forgotten it.

In 2015, a group of rare manuscripts from medieval monasteries went on exhibit at the New York gallery Les Enluminures. The crown jewel of the collection, originally from an abbey in Liesborn, Germany, was a massive handmade book of the four gospels, created for ceremonial purposes such as the swearing of oaths. With its covers crafted from thick oak, the book was ponderously beautiful. The front cover showed Christ on the cross carved in a stunning relief, surrounded by the medieval symbols for the four evangelists: an angel for Matthew, a lion for Mark, an ox for Luke, and an eagle for John. Inside, the text was handwritten in Carolingian minuscule, part of a family of compact script that influenced the development of modern typefaces. (The book was purchased by the Federal Republic of Germany and is back in the abbey, which is now a museum.)

The volume's most unusual attribute was a curious circular diagram on a normally blank protective sheet before the title page. The dealer explained that the drawing had been added when the book was more than a century old. Its concentric bands were filled with spidery writing in deepest brown and brightest red. Small crosses stood sentry at the figure's top and bottom. At the center was the word *DEUS*—God.

The dealer called it the Prayer Wheel.

Since that introduction, the three of us have tracked the Prayer Wheel and its spiritual significance through libraries and archives, with the help of priests, pastors, and scholars, and with some prayer of our own. The Liesborn Wheel is one of about seventy such diagrams surviving from the Middle Ages, a time when there were hundreds or even thousands of them across Europe. They were part of a larger tradition of using geometric figures to represent Christian truths. The great abbot and theologian Richard of St. Victor called the diagrams a "the third mode of seeing."

Outside of a handful of academics, nobody seems to have paid attention to the prayer wheels that remain, buried in a few dozen libraries, private collections, and cathedral archives. But the time has come to change that. As the fruit of an era when tumultuous social conditions resulted in a great flowering of devotion, the Prayer Wheel is also well suited for believers today. It was the prophet Jeremiah who urged a nation under great stress to "ask for the ancient paths . . . and find rest for your souls." The Prayer Wheel shines a light on the old paths to God—and in so doing, can make our praying new again.

A New Promise for Prayer

What is prayer—this running conversation with God—and why do we crave it so? Why do our hearts yearn for communion with something we cannot see, and only sometimes feel?

Christian teachers have long said that prayer is not just a religious imperative but a human reflex. Mother Teresa called it "as necessary as the air, as the blood in our bodies, to keep us alive—to keep us alive to the grace of God."

Yet to flourish, our prayer lives also require tending. We grow and change, after all, and each new generation encounters new challenges. Some of us come from congregations or families that didn't leave us with a sense of ease about personal prayer. Others grew up being told exactly how to pray, yet the formulas now ring hollow, failing to keep pace with our experience or beliefs. Then there are the millions who drift between church traditions, or in and out of the "spiritual but not religious" category. Many today have simply lost touch with any conventional practice of prayer and feel inadequate to the task of starting one of their own.

No wonder that in recent decades, people have found inspiration in monastic practices developed during medieval times and earlier—practices like fixed-hour prayer (also called the divine office), labyrinths (walking prayer), and *lectio divina* (a meditative reading of scripture). The Prayer Wheel is a product of the same monastic communities, in roughly the same period. Like them, the wheel begins with a structured discipline that can seem a little foreign to us at first. But it quickly shows itself to be infinitely adaptable and rewarding. The wheel is almost profligate in the number of doors it opens—new prayers that stimulate more prayers, unexpected insights that touch our parched places, and fresh ways to invite the Spirit into our days.

The wheel could have resurfaced at any time, but it is especially welcome today. It offers prayer prompts boiled down to their most succinct essentials—telegraphic words and phrases that contain multitudes of meaning. In an age when we are shifting from communicating in sentences, paragraphs, and chapters to expressing ideas in a flow of word bites and visual graphics, the wheel offers a bridge between old and new—without compromising substance. Think of it as an early Christian "handheld device," one that is improbably suited to our time. But this device is not yet another distraction—it is something that compels, and rewards, our full attention.

How It Works

The diagram of the wheel we present in this book has four concentric bands each containing a text: the Our Father, a.k.a. the Lord's Prayer (Band 1); Gifts of the Holy Spirit (Band 2); Events in the Life of Christ (Band 3); and the Beatitudes (Band 4). Clearly, the wheel is about these texts, but it's also about how they can relate to and inform one another.

The wheel divides each of the four texts into seven phrases (Eliza's "stepping-stones"). Combined, the twenty-eight phrases offer an entire, compact vocabulary of faith. They address the persons of the Trinity, Jesus' teachings and his role in salvation, heaven and hell, God's kingdom, and more. The result is a remarkable primer in diagram form of what it means to follow Jesus.

Last, the wheel arranges the phrases on the page so that they also reveal the seven contemplative paths toward God. The point is to provide the reader with simple but promising routes to somewhere very important. If Eliza is diligent, if she brings her whole self to the wheel, she will experience a series of unfoldings that lead rapidly and repeatedly to the heart of the faith.

From "Teach Us to Pray" to the Prayer Wheel

This is not the Bible Code. The wheel's paths are not magic, and praying them is not an incantation. Think of it rather as a spiritual "best practice" that grew out of a very old discussion: the one that began when someone made a simple but vital request of Jesus.

The request came after the disciples had watched their leader alone in prayer. "Lord," one of them implored, "teach us to pray."

Jesus' answer, recorded both in Luke and in Matthew, was

'When you pray, say, Our Father, who art in heaven, hallowed [holy] be your name . . ." Only thirty-some words later, the prayer ended. According to both gospels, Jesus also taught his followers briefly about the importance of praying with simplicity, sincerity, and utter trust in their Father's generosity.

Ever since, Christians the world over have cherished Jesus' model conversation with the Father. Catholics came to call the prayer the 'Our Father"; among Protestants, it's known as the "Lord's Prayer." As one second-century Christian wrote, "God alone could teach us how he would have us pray." In the fifth century, Peter Chrysologus exclaimed about the prayer, "The angels stand in awe [of it]. Heaven marvels, earth trembles, flesh does not bear it, hearing does not grasp it, the mind does not penetrate it."

Very quickly, believers came up with various methods to try to extract every particle of meaning from Jesus' prayer. One of the earliest was to divide it into seven phrases, or "petitions," the assumption being that each petition had distinct wisdom to give. Augustine of Hippo (354–430 CE), one of the early Church's most brilliant scholars, went further still: he chose two other beloved texts, divided them into seven phrases apiece as well, and lined those phrases up with the Our Father's seven to invite more insights.

The texts Augustine added were the Beatitudes from Matthew ("the meek shall inherit the earth," et cetera) and the Gifts of the Holy Spirit from the eleventh chapter of the Book of Isaiah (wisdom, fortitude, piety, et cetera). If we were to express his comparison visually, it would be as a grid composed of three horizontal lines divided into sevens. Read horizontally, the chart presents the entirety of each revered text. Read vertically, it aligns the texts' internal parts with one another, exposing new connections between the texts. In this interplay, Augustine found a rich description of the Christian life:

Pray as Jesus taught, and
invite the gifts of his Spirit, then
you can live out the radical virtues he taught in the
    Beatitudes, and
experience the kingdom of God.

After Augustine, more teachers found themselves fascinated with the way in which the three texts commented on one another. By the 800s, an abbot named Paschasius Radbertus had added one more text: the seven events in the life of Christ. The events were a kind of gospel shorthand, combining both the story of Christ from the first three gospels and the Bible's teachings on what it meant to follow him.

Fast-forward two hundred or so years, and something momentous happened: the grid became a wheel. Exactly how and when, no one knows for certain. Perhaps the upgrade in design came because people needed another breakthrough. Spiritual progress often occurs when the world is a mess, just as it had for Augustine, who wrote as the Roman Empire was crumbling around him. When the Prayer Wheel emerged, the era of decay, violence, and chaos sometimes called the Dark Ages had not quite passed. Harvests produced just enough food from year to year, or they didn't. Warfare was a constant. Life could be harsh and short.

Monks and nuns of the era responded by founding new communities and taking literally the directive in 1 Thessalonians 5:17 to "pray without ceasing." If they were working in the fields, they prayed there. They prayed in their chapel in the small hours of the morning. For these communal mystics, the peeling of potatoes with intention and surrender was prayer. In our world, the river of prayer can seem dammed up, but in theirs it jumped its banks and overflowed.

Sometime in the eleventh century, a Benedictine monk or nun

(we don't know which) had the inspiration to grab the ends of Augustine's linear diagram and pull them around until they met. In that way, the horizontals became circles, and the verticals became paths.

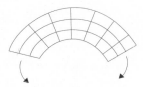

And one more flash of insight: at the center, he or she wrote the word "God." This was the wheel. In the early twelfth century, someone copied it into the gospels book at Liesborn monastery.

The wheel emerged in this world of prayer innovation. And while it was built from the parts of Augustine's grid of Bible verses plus the events of Christ's life, in three crucial ways it was much more.

- *Participation.* The wheel is no longer a study but a tactile experience for believers to enter into. Traces of smudges on the Liesborn version of the wheel suggest the monks were following the paths with their fingers.

- *Organization.* Medieval Christians were fascinated by *ordo,* or order—maybe because their world provided so little of it. *Ordo* could mean the order of prayer, a monastic "order" (or group), or the order of the planets. Most important, it pointed to the grand order of God, in which his people could participate. This way of thinking resulted in the widespread use of geometric forms— rectangles, triangles, circles—to compress and convey data. The Benedictine who pulled Augustine's grid into a circle was illustrating the wholeness and perfection of the Christian message while presenting the gospel texts in a way that was even more accessible for personal devotion.

- *Direction.* In Augustine's version you could compare the scriptural phrases, but there was no destination. In the wheel, the paths reflected and invited the pilgrim's spiritual journey toward God.

In later centuries, people created ever-bigger wheels by adding more sevens: the seven deadly sins, the seven virtues, the seven ways of the Holy Scripture, the seven weapons of spiritual justice, and so on. In the 1200s, a Majorcan named Ramon Llull incorporated sixteen circles in a vast gizmo that one scholar describes as "an irrefutable logical system to convert the heathen."

By the sixteenth century, though, diagrams like the Prayer Wheel seem to have gone out of style. Perhaps the lavishness of some of the later models alienated Protestant reformers. Or perhaps the attraction of diagramming decreased when the printing press made it easy and cheap to employ as many words as you wanted to spread the gospel.

The Wheel Now

The needs of believers today may not be the same as those who created the Prayer Wheel. While the faithful in medieval times likely wanted to deepen an already encompassing prayer life, many people now are searching, sometimes on their own, amid many distractions, for sparks to prevent the inner flame from guttering out.

Fortunately, the wheel is as saturated in the central truths of the faith as it is innovative in their presentation. After a short period of using it in a devotional practice, you'll have its image imprinted on your mind. A store of associations and prayers will accompany t, ready whenever you need them. You will have become familiar with four indispensable texts of the faith, and see more clearly the timeless, soulful paths to which you are called. And you may have initiated a spiritual practice that will stay with you for the rest of your life.

The first part of what follows is a straightforward journey around the wheel: a daily prayer practice that follows the seven paths, starting with the first petition from the Lord's Prayer and ending with the seventh Beatitude. This is one of the best ways to learn and benefit from the spiritual riches of the wheel because it's intuitive and it touches on each of the phrases that make up the paths.

But there are many other possibilities. Part 2 explores ways to pray the wheel topically—for example, during times of special need or celebration. Part 3 offers ways to follow the wheel into the Bible. From there, you're empowered to continue experimenting on your own, perhaps with the added background Part 4 provides about each of the main texts of the wheel. You might want to meditate on a single phrase. You might choose to pray paths with a group and enjoy learning from one another's experiences.

We think you'll find what people like Eliza are finding—that once you begin to pray the wheel, it gets inside you, begins to generate a new conversation with God, and makes every prayer a return home.

PART 1

Seven Paths Through the Prayer Wheel

For each of the next seven weeks, we'll be praying one of the paths, or spokes, of the Prayer Wheel. Since each of the paths is divided into seven phrases, it is easy to pray one phrase a day, moving with intention from the outside to the wheel's center once a week. (Note that each Beatitude occupies two steps on the path— each is split in half, crossing through God in the center.) To help you navigate, each prayer's facing page offers brief reflections on that day's step.

In view of the wheel's invocation ("The order of the diagram . . ."), the first prayer each week is always a prayer of homecoming. It also introduces all the steps you'll take that week.

After that first day, the subsequent steps, and our prayer based on them, follow this pattern:

Day 2:   Petition from the Lord's Prayer
Day 3:   Gift of the Holy Spirit
Day 4:   Event in Christ's life
Day 5:   Beatitude blessing ("Blessed are the . . .")

Day 6:   Beatitude promise (". . . for they will be . . .")

Day 7:   Praying the whole path

Some of the prayers use "I" and "me" language; others use "we" and "us." Feel free to adapt the language for what feels most comfortable for you.

You might find it helpful to trace your finger along the path while you are praying, especially for the first and last days of the week, when you'll be reflecting on every element in the path. Also, you might want to journal as you pray, noting what images, questions, associations, and insights each phrase evokes.

One of the wheel's beautiful mysteries is the way in which the seven paths fit together in one continuous round of prayer. With that in mind, each week ends with a few thoughts on how its path leads into the next path.

WEEK 1

Holy Is Your Name

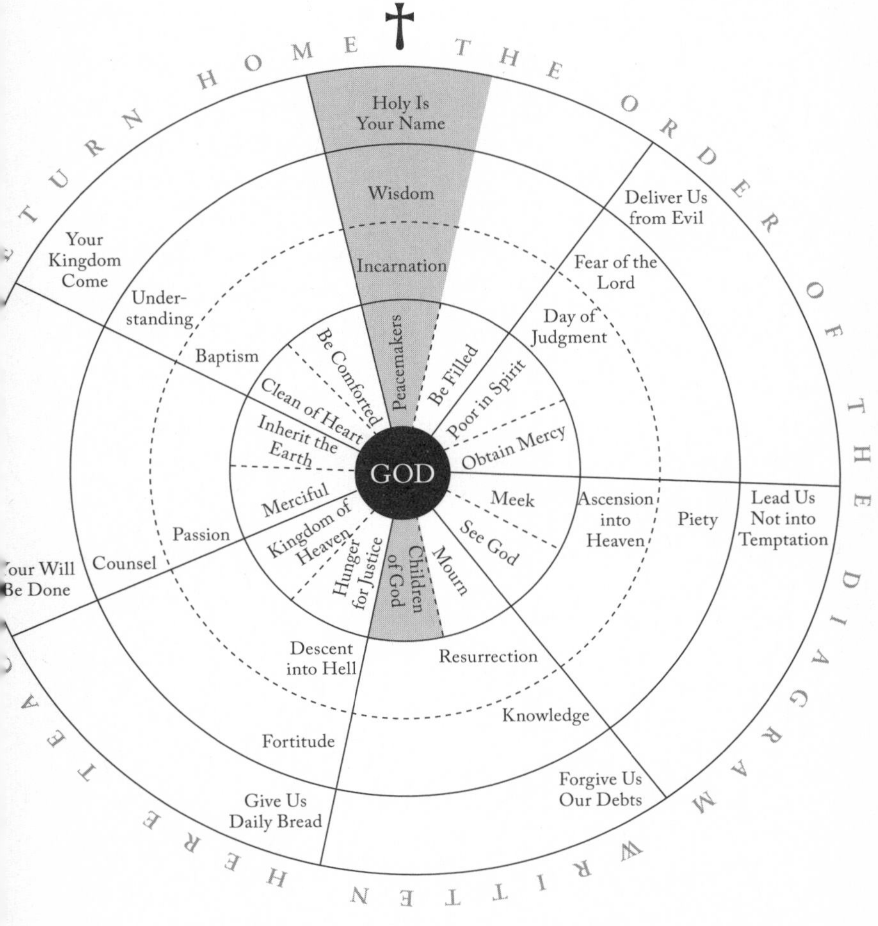
TURN HOME THE ORDER OF THE DIAGRAM WRITTEN HERE TEA
Holy Is Your Name
Wisdom
Incarnation
Peacemakers
Deliver Us from Evil
Fear of the Lord
Day of Judgment
Be Filled
Poor in Spirit
Obtain Mercy
Your Kingdom Come
Under-standing
Baptism
Be Comforted
Clean of Heart
Inherit the Earth
GOD
Meek
Ascension into Heaven
Piety
Lead Us Not into Temptation
Merciful
Passion
Kingdom of Heaven
Hunger for Justice
Children of God
Mourn
See God
our Will Be Done
Counsel
Descent into Hell
Resurrection
Knowledge
Fortitude
Forgive Us Our Debts
Give Us Daily Bread

Stepping into the Path

To you, O Lord, I lift up my soul;
O my God, in you I trust.

PSALM 25:1

The wheel's first path blends together foundational ideas of the faith: who God is, how he relates to us, how we relate to him, and what Christ's followers are called to do and be in the world.

The Lord's Prayer opens with "Our Father in heaven, hallowed [or holy] be your name." When Jesus taught his disciples to begin prayer this way, he named two truths about God's identity: God is as near and dear as a loving father, and he is also as holy and powerful as an almighty king. He's both the creator-ruler of all things and a gentle dad—indeed, the term Jesus uses for "Father" here is more like "Daddy."

Stepping into the Path
Holy Is Your Name
Wisdom
Incarnation
Peacemakers
Children of God

My father in heaven,

From you I come and to you one day I will return.

As I pray this week's path, help me to find my home in you.

◆

Our father in heaven, holy is your name.

◆

As I reflect on the *incarnation* of Jesus, I ask for your *gift of wisdom.*

◆

Blessed are the peacemakers.

◆

For they will be called children of God.

◆

You, O God, are my true home. Amen.

Holy Is Your Name

It is that very Spirit bearing witness with our spirit that we are children of God.

ROMANS 8:16

E arly Christians saw *Holy is your name* as a kind of petition—a request for God to take action. When we pray this line from Jesus' prayer, we're worshipping God in his utter perfection, while at the same time asking God to make the world into the kind of place where divine goodness is manifest to one and all.

Stepping into the Path
Holy Is Your Name
Wisdom
Incarnation
Peacemakers
Children of God

Our father in heaven, holy is your name.

You are "father." And you are "holy."
Help us to live more deeply into this dual reality—
    that you are as near and trustworthy as a loving daddy;
    and that your very nature is flawless beyond imagining.

You are, O Lord, the essence of perfection:
    No one is higher or better.
    Nothing is more sacred.
    You are the source and essence of all life.
    You hold the universe together by your word.
    Even your name is pure and flawless,
    and you hold us, who are not those things, in your sway.

Yet you are a loving parent.
    You give us life and teach us your ways.
    You are tender, protective, generous, and kind.
    When we stray, your whole desire is only for our good.

Show us, your children, how to embrace both your fatherliness
    and your holiness today.

Amen.

⚡ DAY 3

Wisdom

If any of you is lacking in wisdom, ask God, who gives to all generously and ungrudgingly, and it will be given you.

JAMES 1:5

In the Bible, wisdom is the spiritual gift that underlies all other spiritual gifts, the starting point and requirement for living the truly good life. "The wisdom that comes from heaven," wrote the apostle James, "is first pure; then peaceable, gentle, willing to yield, full of mercy and good fruits, without a trace of partiality or hypocrisy" (3:17).

| Stepping into the Path |
| Holy Is Your Name |
| Wisdom |
| Incarnation |
| Peacemakers |
| Children of God |

Holy Spirit,

You have promised to give us wisdom if we ask, and without holding our need against us. You don't fault us for asking, then asking again. I need this gift today.

Grant me deeper understanding in the common things, the things I do out of habit and without a second thought. May every part of my life be infused with your life—like light, like streams of waters.

Help me to rightly examine all things, to discern right from wrong, to see clearly what I should do. I need wisdom in
~my work
~my relationships
~how I speak to others
~how I spend and save money
~how I eat
~what I give my attention to throughout this day

And it's not just for me. In the push and shove of competing opinions, our whole community needs wisdom. Grant us insight in our thoughts and desires, so that our minds can be open, uncluttered, and vibrant. Give us your wisdom, that we may be more like you.

Thank you for this gift.

Amen.

Incarnation

And the Word became flesh and lived among us . . .

JOHN 1:14

The incarnation is one of Christianity's wildest and deepest claims: that the creator of the universe became human in the person of Jesus Christ. God used to live around here, and we knew him, John is saying. At the beginning of a letter that bears his name, John writes that he and his friends had "seen . . . looked at . . . and touched with our hands" the presence of God on the earth (1 John 1:1).

Stepping into the Path
Holy Is Your Name
Wisdom
Incarnation
Peacemakers
Children of God

Lord Jesus,

You were both God and man, together in one being.

You know what it's like to walk down a road. You know what it's like to be hungry. To want things you can't have. To injure yourself, feel pain, and have to wait for healing. To miss someone. To suffer great loss, with nothing but time and prayer to heal the ache.

You know what it's like to see the world as a child, as a teenager, as an adult.

Help me to remember this. There's nothing I'm going through that you don't understand. I don't have any fears or hopes or pains that you can't imagine. You've been there, because you've been here, with us, on this earth, in all its beauty and all its brokenness.

Thank you, Lord Christ, for dwelling among us then, and living with us still.

Amen.

Blessed Are the Peacemakers

And a harvest of righteousness is sown in peace for those who make peace.
JAMES 3:18

This Beatitude appears near last in the Sermon on the Mount in Matthew 5, yet it appears in the Prayer Wheel's first path. Perhaps it was placed here because it brings "children of God" into the same prayer path as "Father."

Tomorrow's prayer connects "children of God" to peacemaking. For today, we speak a blessing over people whose actions bring restoration, healing, and reconciliation in our world.

Stepping into the Path
Holy Is Your Name
Wisdom
Incarnation
Peacemakers
Children of God

Lord,

You said, *Blessed are the peacemakers.*

Help us to become peacemakers. Show us how.
 Where can we show up?
 Where can we be present where there is no peace?
 What conflict do we need to go toward, not run from?
 Where do we need to speak up for reconciliation?
 To whom do we need to listen?
 Where is our opportunity to make peace?

Thank you for those who defend the poor and powerless all over the world today. Thank you for those who devote their lives to the cause of nonviolence, restoration, and healing. May they know the blessing of your comfort and refreshment.

Help us all to notice in our own lives where we can invite and create peace—and nudge us to act.

Amen.

For They Will Be Called Children of God

He said: "Truly I tell you, unless you change and become like children, you will never enter the kingdom of heaven."

MATTHEW 18:3

When suffering continues unabated for individuals and communities, we can become jaded. Today, we pray to become like children—at least in certain important ways. We remember that, in the incarnation, God chose to enter the world as a child—innocent, trusting, humble, and dependent. Jesus' call to childlikeness is an invitation for us to do the same.

Stepping into the Path
Holy Is Your Name
Wisdom
Incarnation
Peacemakers
Children of God

Heavenly Father,

Teach me a child's way of living in my heart and mind today:
    playful
    open
    curious
    unguarded
    innocent
    quick to giggle
    delighted in the moment
    easily contented
    ready to hope—and hope big—all over again
    forgetful of yesterday
    reaching for Mommy
    reaching for Daddy
    reaching often, God—
    secure in your presence
    believing in your goodness
    trusting in your strength

I want to change and become little in my spirit. Teach me what that looks like.

Help me to let go of the grown-up stuff I'm so prideful about, like what I think I know, especially about you.

Remake me like a child in all the right ways, that I may walk in your kingdom today.

Amen.

⫣ DAY 7

Praying the Whole Path

O Lord, you are our Father;
we are the clay, and you are our potter;
we are all the work of your hand.

ISAIAH 64:8

Each week, as you prepare to pray the whole path at once on Day 7, we'll invite you to reflect on the preceding days. This week, consider how your experience relates to the wheel's invocation about returning home to God.

How has your prayer journey this week brought you home?

How were you reminded of who you are, who God is, and where you belong?

Stepping into the Path
Holy Is Your Name
Wisdom
Incarnation
Peacemakers
Children of God

God,

You are holy. May your sacred presence in all people and all living things be known and revered throughout the world.

You are our Father. You care for us as the most loving mothers and fathers care for their children. May we rest today in your care.

You grant wisdom to all who ask. May your wisdom guide us and shape us in all we do. We are all the work of your hand—help us to flourish in insight, common sense, and discretion.

You, Lord Jesus, are the Prince of Peace. Wherever there is strife in the world today—in relationships, in communities, between races and religions, between nations—may peace, not violence, prevail. And may your children be the first to love peace and pursue it, so that we can bring some heaven to earth.

Thank you that none of these requests—nothing we could ever ask or imagine or need—is alien to you, because you know what it is like to be human. Thank you, God, for dwelling among us, and for showing us the way home.

Amen.

Connecting This Path with the Next

As you pray the paths in sequence, you'll often find one path preparing you for the next. At the end of each week, we'll point to some of those connections.

This week, we prayed for wisdom, and next week we'll ask for understanding. Are those two versions of the same thing? Not really.

According to Christian tradition, wisdom helps us to *desire* rightly, while understanding helps us to *decide* rightly. Wisdom forms our hearts to *want* the things of God. Understanding forms our minds to *grasp* the things of God. (See Part 4 for more on the subtle yet important distinctions between the biblical gifts of knowledge, understanding, wisdom, and counsel.)

WEEK 2

Your Kingdom Come

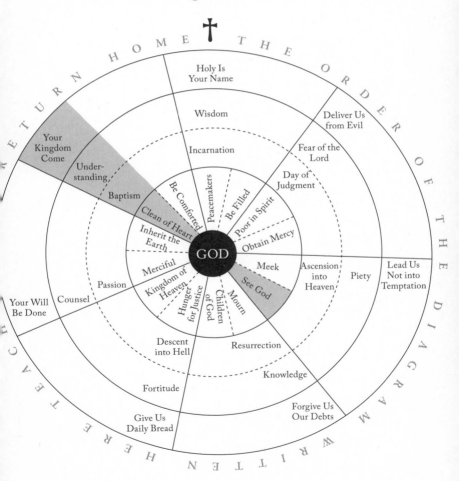

Your Kingdom Come

Understanding

Baptism

Be Comforted

Clean of Heart

Inherit the Earth

Merciful

Passion

Counsel

Your Will Be Done

Kingdom of Heaven

Hunger for Justice

Children of God

Descent into Hell

Fortitude

Give Us Daily Bread

Peacemakers

Be Filled

Poor in Spirit

Obtain Mercy

Meek

See God

Mourn

GOD

Holy Is Your Name

Wisdom

Incarnation

Deliver Us from Evil

Fear of the Lord

Day of Judgment

Ascension into Heaven

Piety

Lead Us Not into Temptation

Resurrection

Knowledge

Forgive Us Our Debts

RETURN HOME · THE ORDER OF THE DIAGRAM WRITTEN HERE TEACH

⚹ DAY 1

Stepping into the Path

Make me to know your ways, O Lord;
teach me your paths.

PSALM 25:4

The second path invites new beginnings. This week, we encounter Jesus' baptism, a scene of renewal. We pray for clean hearts, that we may better see God. And we are grounded in the prayer *your kingdom come*, a kingdom that already exists all around us if only we have eyes to see.

Stepping into the Path
Your Kingdom Come
Understanding
Baptism
Clean of Heart
See God

My father in heaven,

From you I come and to you one day I will return.

As I pray this week's path, help me to find my home in you.

◆

Your kingdom come.

◆

As I meditate on the *baptism* of Jesus, I ask for the *gift of understanding.*

◆

Blessed are the clean of heart.

◆

For they will see God.

◆

You, O God, are my true home. Amen.

⤳ DAY 2

Your Kingdom Come

Once Jesus was asked by the Pharisees when the kingdom of God was coming, and he answered, "The kingdom of God is not coming with things that can be observed; nor will they say, 'Look, here it is!' or 'There it is!' For, in fact, the kingdom of God is among you."

LUKE 17:20–21

Jesus' entire ministry—what he taught and how he lived—was a revelation of God's kingdom. Many of his parables were framed as descriptions of it—"The kingdom of God is like," he would begin, then tell a story of the search for a treasured item or a farmer planting seed. In some of his stories, the points seemed clear; at other times, he left his listeners to puzzle through their meanings.

Consistently, though, Jesus taught that the kingdom reality he spoke of exists not only as God's perfected order in the future but also in the here and now, whenever people awaken to God's presence and intentions for the world.

Stepping into the Path
Your Kingdom Come
Understanding
Baptism
Clean of Heart
See God

Lord God,

Your kingdom seems far away today. We see death and disaster in the news, and everywhere, people are arguing, always arguing. And yet Jesus said that your domain—the only true and enduring reality—is also among us.

May your kingdom come in the middle of our despair.

Even in my own heart, I hold grudges, nurse anxieties, withhold compassion, and put myself first. Too often, my heart is not a hospitable place for your Spirit. I resist your rightful rule there, too.

May your kingdom come first in my heart.

Empower your people to see where your way of life is already showing up. Help us to become passionate agents in this continuing unfolding of your will for all things.

Amen.

Understanding

If you indeed cry out for insight,
and raise your voice for understanding;
if you seek it like silver,
and search for it as for hidden treasures—
then you will understand the fear of the Lord
and find the knowledge of God.

PROVERBS 2:3–5

T o pray for understanding is to ask for a calm and welcoming receptivity so that we may penetrate the surface of things and get to the depths. The first step of understanding is recognizing how much we don't know, and how limited our perspective can be.

That's a good posture anytime we come before God: receptive to his thoughts above our own, wanting his perspective to seep into and overtake ours. The gift of understanding allows us to glimpse God's point of view.

| Stepping into the Path |
| Your Kingdom Come |
| Understanding |
| Baptism |
| Clean of Heart |
| See God |

Holy Spirit,

You've promised the gift of understanding. Yet I am so often blind to your presence, your will, and your ways.

Teach me to see you and live. I cry out today for help to see beyond my limitations.

Teach me to seek for understanding as if it were a buried treasure that's waiting and available to me if I keep digging, keep asking.

Show me your presence, your will, and your ways—in the scriptures, in my ordinary day, in the starfish fingers of a newborn, in the beauty of faith.

Hear my cry for insight.

Amen.

Baptism

In those days Jesus came from Nazareth of Galilee and was baptized by John in the Jordan. And just as he was coming up out of the water, he saw the heavens torn apart and the Spirit descending like a dove on him. And a voice came from heaven, "You are my Son, the Beloved; with you I am well pleased."

MARK 1:9–11

No one who sensed Jesus' divinity would've expected him to show up for the repentance ritual of baptism. John the Baptizer exclaimed in amazement, "I need to be baptized by you, and do you come to me?" But John relented, and as Jesus came up out of the water, the heavens cracked open and God spoke.

The Greek word used here for the heavens opening conveys considerable violence. In the life of a Christian, baptism upends the life we once had. We go under the water as an act of repentance and dying to self, and we rise to begin a new life in the Spirit.

Stepping into the Path
Your Kingdom Come
Understanding
Baptism
Clean of Heart
See God

Father in heaven,

I turn from all that's old and past today,
    I turn from self and sin,
    and turn with all my heart to you.

Free me from my old ideas, my lesser self,
    my prideful determination
    to make my own way in the world.
    That was the way of death, not life.
    I let it all go.

Raise me up from these waters
    to a new forever life in Jesus.
    By your salvation, make me new
    that I may faithfully follow Christ the Lord.

Father, I belong to you now.
    Open the heavens to declare
    your love and your delight today
    in me, your new-washed child.

Amen.

Blessed Are the Clean of Heart

Let us approach with a true heart in full assurance
of faith, with our hearts sprinkled clean from an evil
conscience and our bodies washed with pure water.

HEBREWS 10:22

The association between baptism and "clean of heart" is beautifully intuitive. Sin and self distort our view of God. Baptism washes sin and guilt away, freeing us to see God without that misunderstanding. In light of this freedom, we can move past our own limitations and begin to see God at work in our world.

Stepping into the Path
Your Kingdom Come
Understanding
Baptism
Clean of Heart
See God

Lord,

Create in me each day a clean heart, and renew my attitudes and priorities. Keep me in your presence, and preserve my soul with your Holy Spirit. Restore in me a daily gratitude for new life in God, and that moment when I first understood that I belonged to you.

That's what the Psalmist prayed many centuries ago (Psalm 51), and it's the cry of my heart today. It's also the cry of all who follow you, and I join my prayer to theirs.

We are yours, Lord. Shape our affections and loyalties to reflect and honor our higher calling in the world. On this road of repentance, make us true disciples and heralds of the good news of your kingdom.

Thank you that I can come to you "in full assurance of faith." Thank you for hearing and answering the cry of my heart.

Amen.

For They Shall See God

For now we see in a mirror, dimly, but then we will see face to face. Now I know only in part; then I will know fully, even as I have been fully known.

1 CORINTHIANS 13:12

H ere at the end of the path, the final promise—that we "shall see God"—comes full circle with the opening petition, *Your kingdom come*. Clean and clear-sighted, we can see God *and* God's activity all around us. Here is the kingdom. Here is the promised new life, where we are already known and welcomed.

Stepping into
the Path

Your Kingdom
Come

Understanding

Baptism

Clean of Heart

See God

Lord Jesus,

We look forward to that moment when someday we'll see you face-to-face, like a mother looks forward to finally gazing upon the face of her newborn child.

Guide us toward that moment of union more fully each day, and in the meantime, open our eyes to see glimpses of you all around.

Teach us to recognize the ways that your Spirit is at work in our world, and cleanse our inner being so that we may fully receive you.

Blessed are the clean of heart, for they shall see God. Today, we rest in the confidence of knowing we *will* see you.

Amen.

Praying the Whole Path

So, if anyone is in Christ, there is a new creation: everything old has passed away; see, everything has become new!

2 CORINTHIANS 5:17

This week brought us to the waters of baptism and opened our spiritual eyes to new understandings.

Where do you see God's kingdom, his new way of being, coming in your life or in the world around you?

Stepping into the Path
Your Kingdom Come
Understanding
Baptism
Clean of Heart
See God

Heavenly Father,

Today I seek not the passing rewards of recognition, power, and wealth, but your kingdom of love and justice. I turn again from self to follow the way of Jesus.

So, Father, may your kingdom come—in this world and in my life.

Direct my intentions and energies to the higher, enduring reality springing up all around me, pushing back the darkness. I'm desperate to discern where your Spirit is moving.

So, Father, give me your gift of understanding.

Even as I contemplate the kingdom Jesus came to announce, I am conscious of my own weakness and need. I want to stay on your path, but it's easy to lose my way.

So, Father, remind me of the cleansing waters of baptism and the moment I first understood I was your beloved child. Remove the scales from my eyes, so that I can better see you.

Thank you, Father, that today I am made new in you.

Amen.

Connecting This Path with the Next

If the second path can be summed up by the theme of new beginnings (baptism, cleanliness, and fresh eyes for the kingdom), the third invites us to consider what might naturally come next—for example, what it means to be God's hands and feet in the world.

The second path's focus on baptism also prepares us for something key to the third: Christ's suffering and death. At our baptism we symbolically died to our old way of life. When we rise again, wet with grace, it's a foreshadowing of the glory of resurrection.

WEEK 3

Your Will Be Done

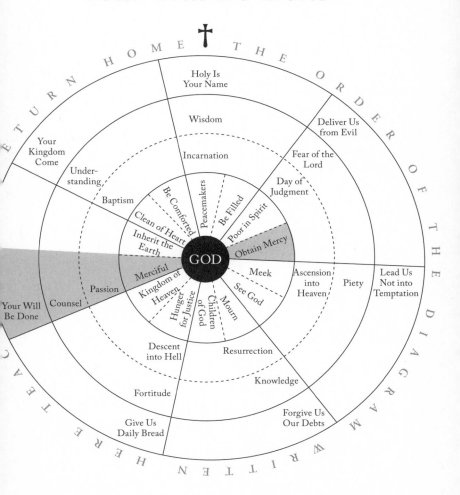

RETURN HOME · THE ORDER OF THE DIAGRAM WRITTEN HERE LEA

Holy Is
Your Name

Wisdom

Incarnation

Your
Kingdom
Come

Under-
standing

Baptism

Deliver Us
from Evil

Fear of the
Lord

Day of
Judgment

Be Comforted

Peacemakers

Be Filled

Clean of Heart

Poor in Spirit

Inherit the
Earth

Obtain Mercy

GOD

Meek

Merciful

See God

Ascension
into
Heaven

Lead Us
Not into
Temptation

Piety

Kingdom of
Heaven

Passion

Children
of God

Mourn

Counsel

Hunger
for Justice

Your Will
Be Done

Descent
into Hell

Resurrection

Knowledge

Fortitude

Forgive Us
Our Debts

Give Us
Daily Bread

⚝ DAY 1

Stepping into the Path

Then he said to them all, "If any want to become my followers, let them deny themselves and take up their cross daily and follow me."

LUKE 9:23

Because of the third path's focus on Christ's passion—his experience of betrayal, suffering, and death—it draws us to consider the pain life brings while inviting us to respond as Jesus ultimately did, setting aside our own will in favor of the Father's. And the path culminates in the light of mercy, a transforming gift that we can offer to others and ourselves.

Stepping into the Path
Your Will Be Done
Counsel
Passion
Merciful
Obtain Mercy

My father in heaven,

From you I come and to you one day I will return.

As I pray this week's path, help me to find my home in you.

◆

Your will be done.

◆

As I reflect on the *passion* of Jesus, lead my thoughts and shape my
life by your *gift of counsel.*

◆

Blessed are the merciful.

◆

For they will obtain mercy.

◆

You, O God, are my true home. Amen.

⤳ DAY 2

Your Will Be Done

"Whoever does the will of God is my brother and sister and mother."

MARK 3:35

The words "your will be done" are far easier for us to say than to live. They assume that we're capable of understanding what God's will is, but also that we will not run in the other direction when we know what it requires. Saying "your will be done" means we are asking God, "Take my one brief life, and use me to create a piece of heaven on earth."

Stepping into the Path
Your Will Be Done
Counsel
Passion
Merciful
Obtain Mercy

God of all that is good,

When I look around this world, I see great beauty—echoes of heaven, evidence of every good and perfect gift.

But I also see terrible pain—broken relationships, abused power, malnourished children. And so I pray . . .

May your will be done today, on earth as it is in heaven, and let it begin with me.

Loving Father, Caring Mother, grant me strength to be an instrument of your goodness. Show me what to do and how to do it.

May your will be done today, on earth as it is in heaven, and let it begin with me.

Give us, your people, the conviction to do more than just pray *your will be done*—as though it were happening outside of us, and carried out by other people. Let this be our most heartfelt desire and deepest personal commitment.

Yes, may your will be done today, on earth as it is in heaven, and may it begin with me.

Amen.

Counsel

But the Advocate, the Holy Spirit, whom the Father
will send in my name, will teach you everything,
and remind you of all that I have said to you.

JOHN 14:26

Shortly before Jesus' death, he promised his disciples that even in his absence they would not be alone. God would send them the Holy Spirit to guide them every day. The Spirit is also known as the Advocate, the Comforter, and the Counselor.

The gift of counsel equips us to hear the Spirit's promptings about what to do, where to go, and how to act.

Stepping into the Path
Your Will Be Done
Counsel
Passion
Merciful
Obtain Mercy

Lord Christ,

We are easily confused and uncertain about what to do next. Thank you for the divine Counselor, the Holy Spirit.

We call upon your Holy Spirit to fill our hearts and direct our desires.

We call upon your Holy Spirit to open our inner ears to your still, small voice.

We call upon your Holy Spirit to help us discern your ways and accomplish your will in our world.

Teach and remind us that God's will is also our best and highest good. Counsel us in the way of Jesus today and every day.

Grant all those who call on you the strength to know your will and carry it out, whatever the cost. And grant us your peace as we follow you.

Amen.

Passion

While Jesus was going up to Jerusalem, he took the twelve disciples aside by themselves, and said to them on the way, "See, we are going up to Jerusalem, and the Son of Man will be handed over to the chief priests and scribes, and they will condemn him to death; then they will hand him over to the Gentiles to be mocked and flogged and crucified; and on the third day he will be raised."

MATTHEW 20:17–19

Jesus not only taught his followers to pray for God's will but showed them what doing it looked like, especially during his final, heart-rending days. Christians refer to this time as Christ's passion, celebrated during Holy Week. The week begins with Palm Sunday and Jesus' triumphant entry into Jerusalem, follows him through betrayal by his own disciples on Maundy Thursday, and his crucifixion on Good Friday, before culminating in his resurrection on Easter morning.

On the night before he was crucified, Jesus prayed through tears, "Father, if you are willing, remove this cup from me; yet, not my will but yours be done." Whatever we face, the Spirit can help us. It might be to discover a purpose in the suffering (if it is there to be found), or show us a way out, or give us strength to surrender to a greater will.

Stepping into the Path
Your Will Be Done
Counsel
Passion
Merciful
Obtain Mercy

Lord Jesus,

How confused and disappointed your disciples must have been when you told them that you were about to suffer and die. That wasn't how they imagined their journey with you would end.

We, too, are so often surprised by pain and suffering. It feels somehow wrong—a terrible mistake. We feel born for another life.

Yet we are grateful that you chose to show the way to life through suffering. In our times of sorrow, loss, and pain, we look to you, who has gone before. Thank you that you understand when we balk, want to turn back, escape, find another way.

Teach us how to suffer well. Fill us with courage and grant us strength to take the bitter with the sweet. Strengthen all your people to face what lies ahead today: health problems, financial hardships, broken relationships, fear, and want—whatever life brings. And, especially, be a refuge and a solace for those around the world who face imprisonment, persecution, violence, and death.

Even in our suffering, may your will be done. Even in our suffering, you are worthy to be praised. And today we praise your name.

Amen.

Blessed Are the Merciful

For we do not have a high priest who is unable to sympathize with our weaknesses, but we have one who in every respect has been tested as we are, yet without sin. Let us therefore approach the throne of grace with boldness, so that we may receive mercy and find grace to help in time of need.

HEBREWS 4:15–16

We began this path by praying for God's will to be done. Here's one way to do it: be merciful. We might even say that God's will cannot be done without mercy.

We are merciful when we refuse to do harm to someone, even and especially when we know we are in the right. When people mistreat us or disappoint us, and we respond with love and kindness instead of retribution, we are following Christ's example and manifesting God's nature in the world.

| Stepping into the Path |
| Your Will Be Done |
| Counsel |
| Passion |
| Merciful |
| Obtain Mercy |

Jesus the Christ,

When you were on the cross, naked and alone,
    when they drove the nails in your body,
    during the hours of agony they made you suffer,
    you could have called down fire on them
    to avenge yourself right then and there,
    punishing every person who beat or mocked you.
    You could have found a way of escape.

But you didn't, Lord. You stayed and prayed
    for your tormentors.
    You asked, "Father, forgive them;
    for they do not know what they are doing."
    They deserved payback, but on their behalf,
    you begged God for mercy.

That's how I know God is strong.
    That's how I know God is loving.
    You could have lashed out in anger and self-righteousness.
    But instead, you chose compassion, grace, mercy—
    even for those who weren't aware they needed it.
    And that one act is still redeeming the world.

Your mercy, Jesus—what a beautiful gift!
    What an amazing response of strength!
    Bless me and all who follow you
    with your beautiful, transforming gift of mercy today,
    that we, too, may participate in your saving work in the world.

Amen.

For They Shall Obtain Mercy

For judgment will be without mercy to anyone who has shown no mercy; mercy triumphs over judgment.

JAMES 2:13

Paradoxically, the way to receive mercy is to give it; the way to invite compassion is to pour it out for others. Through our acts of mercy, we do God's will in one little corner of the world, and in so doing, we open ourselves up to receiving divine grace.

Stepping into the Path
Your Will Be Done
Counsel
Passion
Merciful
Obtain Mercy

Heavenly Father,

Yesterday I prayed for mercy, but today I need to ask all over again.

Judgment comes easily for me. Resentment sticks to me like an old habit. But compassion and forgiveness are slow to occur to me—when they occur at all.

Sometimes I forget you said, "Forgive us our debts, *as we forgive our debtors*," and "Blessed are the merciful, *for they will receive mercy.*"

Teach me your whole truth. I so desperately need your mercy, Lord! And remake me as an angel of mercy—an uncalculating, open-handed distributor of your extravagant grace.

May mercy become my first impulse, and *for their sake,* not mine. And thank you for the mercies upon mercies you show me every day.

Amen.

Praying the Whole Path

He has told you, O mortal, what is good;
and what does the Lord require of you
but to do justice, and to love kindness,
and to walk humbly with your God?

MICAH 6:8

Pause for a moment to reflect on the gift of counsel and the blessing of mercy.

What choices are you facing that require special discernment?

What choices, actions, or relationships call for mercy?

Where do you hope for and need mercy for yourself?

Stepping into the Path
Your Will Be Done
Counsel
Passion
Merciful
Obtain Mercy

Heavenly Father,

I stand before you filled with hope. I'm hopeful even when this world seems very dark, because you've said that your will could be done right here, on earth as it is in heaven.

May your will be done.

Teach me to discern your will by the counsel of the Holy Spirit. Awaken me to your guiding light.

Grant me the gift of counsel.

Teach me to understand that Jesus himself suffered not only for my salvation but also because he was human, and that suffering is not a cup that passes from us in this life.

Keep revealing to me the deep truths of Christ's passion.

Teach me to love kindness as much as I love to be fairly treated. Turn me into a champion of mercy when I'd rather make a show of strength. I want to humbly follow the higher, better way of Jesus.

Father, teach me to show mercy, that I may also receive mercy.

Amen.

Connecting This Path with the Next

When we pray things like "your will be done" or "your kingdom come," as we have in the previous two weeks, God often asks us to play a part in the answer. The fourth path combines a prayer for daily bread with a blessing for those who hunger for justice, which we can take as another invitation to move beyond our personal needs to the needs of others. The gift of the fourth path—which is fortitude, or strength—equips us not only to endure suffering but also to hunger for and build a better world.

WEEK 4

Give Us This Day Our Daily Bread

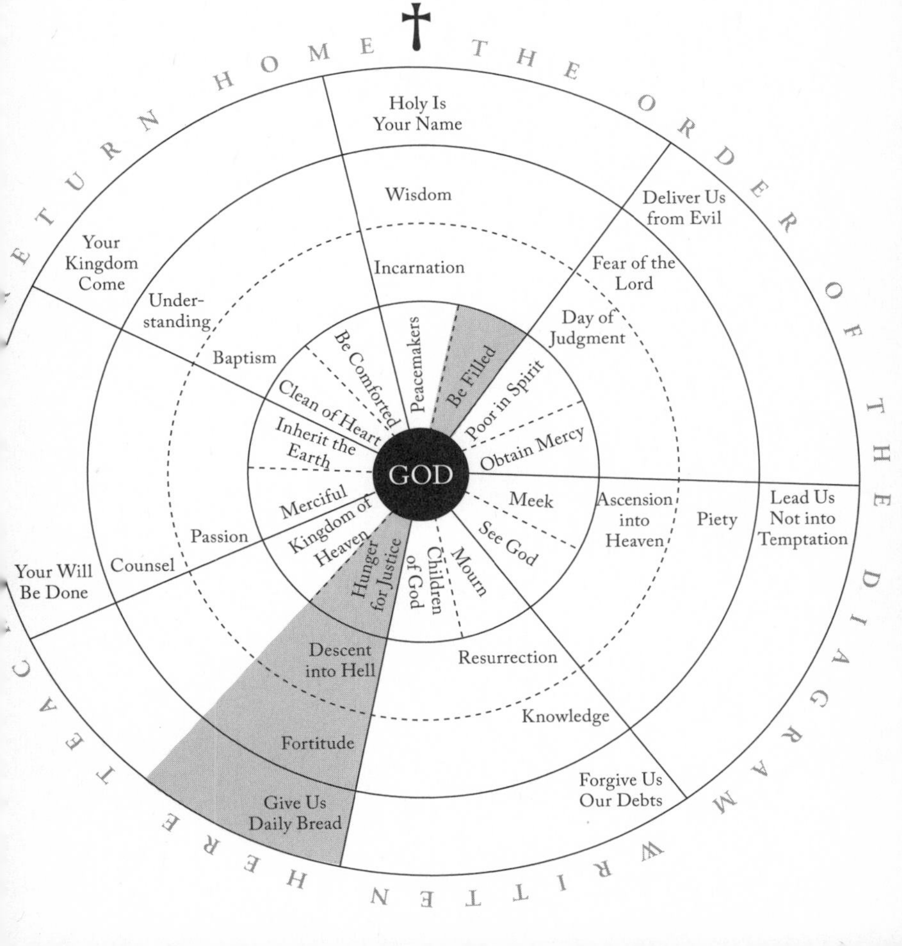

RETURN HOME THE ORDER OF THE DIAGRAM WRITTEN HERE TEACH
Holy Is Your Name
Deliver Us from Evil
Lead Us Not into Temptation
Forgive Us Our Debts
Give Us Daily Bread
Your Will Be Done
Your Kingdom Come
Wisdom
Fear of the Lord
Piety
Knowledge
Fortitude
Counsel
Under-standing
Incarnation
Day of Judgment
Ascension into Heaven
Resurrection
Descent into Hell
Passion
Baptism
Peacemakers
Be Filled
Poor in Spirit
Obtain Mercy
Meek
See God
Mourn
Children of God
Hunger for Justice
Kingdom of Heaven
Merciful
Inherit the Earth
Clean of Heart
Be Comforted
GOD

✣ DAY 1

Stepping into the Path.

Consider my affliction and my trouble.

PSALM 25:18

This fourth path turns our attention to our most pressing needs. Whatever our circumstances, humans need food, shelter, safety for ourselves and our loved ones, health, justice, and daily help for whatever lies ahead. A loving God invites us to bring all these concerns into our conversation with him.

Stepping into the Path
Give Us Daily Bread
Fortitude
Descent into Hell
Hunger for Justice
Be Filled

My father in heaven,

From you I come and to you one day I will return.

As I pray this week's path, help me to find my home in you.

◆

Give us this day our daily bread.

◆

Strengthen me as I reflect on Jesus' *descent into hell* and remember my own darkest struggles.

◆

Blessed are those who hunger for justice.

◆

For they will be filled.

◆

You, O God, are my true home. Amen.

Give Us This Day Our Daily Bread

Jesus said to them, "I am the bread of life. Whoever comes to me will never be hungry, and whoever believes in me will never be thirsty."

JOHN 6:35

All living things need daily sustenance. For humans, that physical need is a spiritual reminder that we depend wholly on God. This prayer evokes the deeper needs of heart, mind, and soul—as Jesus said, "One does not live by bread alone, but by every word that comes from the mouth of God."

| Stepping into the Path |
| Give Us Daily Bread |
| Fortitude |
| Descent into Hell |
| Hunger for Justice |
| Be Filled |

Lord,

Give us this day our daily bread.

May this simple prayer flourish in my heart and mind today. Let it teach me how wholly dependent I am on you for the basics, and how I can trust you for my needs.

Jesus, you asked us to ask.

For the millions who have too little to eat today, have mercy. May all those in positions of power and abundance have mercy, too— mercy that provides for those in need. Show me my necessary part in your provision so those who need food and water can live in health, safety, and dignity.

Jesus, you told us to give.

For the spiritually hungry—may they find deep nourishment in the bread of life. Be present to everyone whose soul is aching. Satisfy and sustain them.

Jesus, only you are the bread of life.

You, Lord, are our provider *and* our provision. You can give me everything I need. And you *are* everything I need.

Amen.

Fortitude

He gives power to the faint,
and strengthens the powerless.

ISAIAH 40:29

"Fortitude" is an old-fashioned word for strength, and a prayer for strength flows quite naturally from yesterday's request for sustenance. Jesus prayed for fortitude in the face of intense strife and suffering. He also prayed for the endurance to fulfill his mission. Likewise, each of us needs strength in times of crisis but also strength to stay faithful to our commitments, and some days, to simply hang on.

Stepping into the Path
Give Us Daily Bread
Fortitude
Descent into Hell
Hunger for Justice
Be Filled

O God,

You promise to give power to the weak.

Where I am weak, grant me the gift of fortitude. Make me strong today. Set me free.

Where I am ignorant of my weakness, lead me gently to see my need for you.

For all your people, I pray:

Strengthen our minds, that we may overcome apathy and ignorance.

Strengthen our spirits, that we may rise above exhaustion and opposition.

Strengthen our hearts, that we may never be mastered by fear.

You are calling all your people to lives of meaning and purpose—lives you can bless; lives that glorify you.

Fill us with energy and endurance by your Spirit, that we may accomplish all that you have given us to do, today and every day.

Amen.

Descent into Hell

If I ascend to heaven, you are there; if I make my bed in Sheol, you are there.

PSALM 139:8

Every Sunday, millions of Christians around the world recite the Apostles' Creed. About halfway through, they intone the curious line "he descended to the dead," a statement that alludes to an ancient belief about Jesus' victory over death and hell. This occurred, it was thought, between the time of his crucifixion and his resurrection, when he overturned the finality of hell to bring salvation to the righteous who had already died before his coming. Major artworks from medieval times depict this as Jesus' "harrowing of hell."

Stepping into the Path
Give Us Daily Bread
Fortitude
Descent into Hell
Hunger for Justice
Be Filled

Lord,

There is nowhere I can go where you would not find me. You took on the darkness of hell itself to rescue humanity from sin and death.

Loving God, find me in my dark places today.

Find me when I am stuck in sin, doing the same thing over and over, even though I know it's bad for me, hurtful to others, and against your will.

Find me when I feel scared of life, fearful about my future, overwhelmed with all I'm facing. Find me when it feels like life is out of control.

If you descended into hell, then surely you are with me on my darkest days. Surely you can bring light even here.

You sustain me when all my resources are gone. You are my strength when I have none. You are the one who rescues me, again and again, and sets me free.

Grant me courage to believe, and to go on. Thank you that nothing I face today, nowhere I go, no deed I've done can separate me from your saving love.

Amen.

✴ DAY 5

Blessed Are Those Who Hunger for Justice

For the Lord your God is God of gods and Lord of lords, the great God, mighty and awesome, who is not partial and takes no bribe, who executes justice for the orphan and the widow, and who loves the strangers, providing them food and clothing.

DEUTERONOMY 10:17–18

Throughout his ministry, Jesus called people's attention away from the comfortable and toward those who lived in dire need. Likewise, this path opens with a prayer for bread and ends with a Beatitude comparing injustice to hunger. There's a blessing, Jesus says, when we hunger after justice and humane provision for all who are deprived and oppressed.

Stepping into the Path
Give Us Daily Bread
Fortitude
Descent into Hell
Hunger for Justice
Be Filled

Father,

Blessed are those who hunger for justice.

In your mercy, Lord, remember those who are desperate, exhausted, beaten down, and forgotten today.

Remember those who are unfairly imprisoned.

Remember those who have limited opportunities, who see no chance to make things better.

Remember those born into failed families, neighborhoods, nations. Remember those growing up in broken circumstances of all kinds. Remember the widow and the orphan.

Remember those whose lives are torn apart by war, or racism, or religious persecution, or unfair laws that prevent them from building a life for themselves and their families.

In your sight, they are my mother and father, my sister and brother, and I am their keeper.

You have called them blessed. Help them to hear your surprising word today. Bless them. Provide for their deepest hungers. Show me my part in that provision, and help me to act on it, for your glory and the welfare of your people.

Amen.

For They Will Be Filled

When justice is done, it is a joy to the righteous,
but dismay to evildoers.

PROVERBS 21:15

For all who suffer deprivation, this week's Beatitude also comes with a promise, one that reads like a prophecy, or a declaration of what is coming: *They will be filled*. Somehow, somewhere, some way, these very ones will enjoy a banquet of justice. They will get to inhabit a world where all is put right.

Stepping into the Path
Give Us Daily Bread
Fortitude
Descent into Hell
Hunger for Justice
Be Filled

Lord,

You want to set the world right. You want to see hungry people have enough food, hurting people receive comfort, endangered people find peace. And we believe you will do it—for you are a God of justice.

Those who hunger for justice will be filled.

We pray now for people in crisis of all kinds. For those who are a phone call or job posting or court decree or timely gift away from turning their lives around. Sustain them, Lord, and may they see their basic rights honored soon.

We pray also for those whose hunger for justice will only grow. For those whose deliverance is a long time away, bring hope and comfort today. Carry them in your grace and mercy. Let them know your love.

They will be filled, because you have promised that they will be. Soon, O God, may it be soon!

And make us part of that filling. May your justice bring us joy. Open our eyes and rekindle our convictions. Show us where we can make things right. And give us the courage to act.

Amen.

Praying the Whole Path

"For the bread of God is that which comes down from heaven and gives life to the world."

JOHN 6:33

From a prayer for sustenance, to a reaching for the gift of strength and endurance, to a blessing for justice, this week brought us closer to understanding our needs and the needs of the world around us.

What does it look like for God to meet your needs?

How about your neighbor's needs, or the needs of someone you know who is in trouble?

Stepping into the Path
Give Us Daily Bread
Fortitude
Descent into Hell
Hunger for Justice
Be Filled

Lord Christ,

Thank you for the *hunger* that is God-given. You created us to work, to play, to love, to give, to dream, to desire.

Provide for our daily necessities—you are the very *bread* of life—and help us to open ourselves to receive what you are holding out to us, even now.

Nourish us in every way. With your gift of *fortitude,* steady our walk and reenergize our determination. Help us to fix our gaze on what matters first and most.

Finally, Lord, be with us when it feels like we or those we love are *descending into hell*—when abandonment, devastation, or death looms. You've walked that path—you know our pain and fear.

Help all your people to stand with those who hunger for justice. Show us how to champion and even to become your provision in their lives.

You have promised that *all who hunger will be filled*. What a mystery! What a hope! Thank you, gracious God, that you are the Bread of Life, given freely to everyone. Today we open our deepest selves to receive your blessing.

Amen.

Connecting This Path with the Next

Praying for daily bread and continual fortitude in the fourth path is a humble admission to God, "I need you." It's good practice for making ourselves comfortable with the notion—and the reality—that we are creatures who rely on our Creator for every breath. It helps us to right-size our estimations of ourselves.

The next path begins with "Forgive us our debts," a plea that applies to everyone. None of us escape the ongoing need to seek forgiveness for the things we do, say, or think.

But, as we'll see, forgiveness opens a window in our hearts. New life springs up. Even in our mourning, we can glimpse an ultimate and everlasting comfort.

WEEK 5

Forgive Us Our Debts

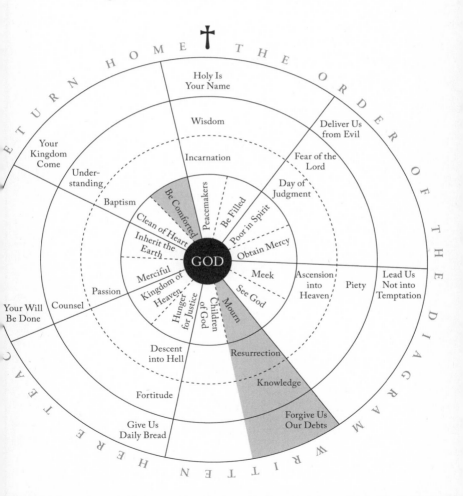

Stepping into the Path

"I will get up and go to my father, and I will say to him, 'Father, I have sinned against heaven and before you; I am no longer worthy to be called your son; treat me like one of your hired hands.' So he set off and went to his father. But while he was still far off, his father saw him and was filled with compassion; he ran and put his arms around him and kissed him."

LUKE 15:18–20

Though the petition *Forgive us our debts* comes near the end of the Lord's Prayer, many church traditions place that confession at the beginning of the service. Perhaps that's because, as with the prodigal son, our sins can leave us feeling unworthy of the Father's affection.

This week's path, like all true journeys to God, does not keep us stuck in our guilt. From absolution, it leads us to resurrection and the promise of comfort.

| Stepping into the Path |
| Forgive Us Our Debts |
| Knowledge |
| Resurrection |
| Mourn |
| Be Comforted |

My father in heaven,

From you I come and to you one day I will return.

As I pray this week's path, help me to find my home in you.

◆

Forgive us our debts, as we forgive our debtors.

◆

As I remember the *resurrection* of Jesus, help me grow in the *gift of knowledge.*

◆

Blessed are those who mourn.

◆

For they will be comforted.

◆

You, O God, are my true home. Amen.

Forgive Us Our Debts

Happy are those whose transgression is forgiven,
whose sin is covered.

PSALM 32:1

"Forgive us our debts" points to the whole expression in Jesus' prayer: "Forgive us our debts (sins), as we also have forgiven our debtors." Thinking of sin as a moral debt is less common in our time, but this prayer inspires us to remember that forgiveness is not just something we need, but something we owe to those who have wronged us. The gospel spreads mercy to everyone.

Stepping into the Path
Forgive Us Our Debts
Knowledge
Resurrection
Mourn
Be Comforted

Loving Father,

We ask you to forgive our debts, as we forgive our debtors. Over and over, you hear your children pray for forgiveness for the same old thing. Yet you have said that your mercies never come to an end—that they are new every morning.

These sins against you and others weigh on my conscience today:

[Pause for reflection and confession.]

Please forgive me of all these wrongs. Make me new, clean, and debt free, by your grace. Thank you, Lord.

And please help me now to also forgive everyone who has harmed me. These sins against me by others have weighed on my heart and stolen my serenity:

[Pause for reflection and confession.]

Please help me forgive all wrongdoers their wrongs. I release them now. I toss their debts into the sea of forgetting. Thank you, Lord.

Teach me to live anew today in the freedom of being pardoned and of granting pardon.

Amen.

Knowledge

An intelligent mind acquires knowledge,
and the ear of the wise seeks knowledge.

PROVERBS 18:15

The gift of knowledge is paired here with Christ's resurrection, the ultimate fact of history for all Christians. This pairing suggests that the gift of knowledge is an ability to know deeply what we might call the "facts of God." Some facts strike us nearly speechless with awe. Others seem counterintuitive, if not impossible—including the idea that a person could die and then live again.

Stepping into the Path
Forgive Us Our Debts
Knowledge
Resurrection
Mourn
Be Comforted

Lord God,

Graciously grant me the spirit of knowledge today.
    Fill me with knowledge when the air is thick with ideas,
    and I don't know whom to believe.
    Fill me with knowledge when I am plagued by worries.
    Help me to hand them over to you
    so there's room in my mind
    for truer, better thoughts and feelings.

Grant me your spirit of knowledge that I may
    trust you completely, and rest in that trust.

Fill all those who call on you
    with the same spirit of knowledge that led Jesus,
    that helped him know what to say, what to think, what to do.

Yes, may your spirit of knowledge
    shine out from our innermost beings,
    that we may know and share your presence,
    your nature,
    and your will at work in the world around us.

Amen.

Resurrection

*I want to know Christ and the power of his resurrection and
the sharing of his sufferings by becoming like him in his death,
if somehow I may attain the resurrection from the dead.*

PHILIPPIANS 3:10–11

If you could trust in only one miracle described in the Bible, this
is the one: that Jesus died, was buried, and, on the third day, rose
again. Most Christians believe this event happened, but what's
harder is to take the resurrection seriously every day—to make
God's power over death a way of life.

Jesus' resurrection is God's announcement that the world has
begun to change. All that is dead will be brought to life. All that is
broken is being made whole.

| Stepping into the Path |
| Forgive Us Our Debts |
| Knowledge |
| Resurrection |
| Mourn |
| Be Comforted |

Lord Jesus,

Today, I pray with Paul that you would help me to know the power of your resurrection.

Help me to know it not just factually but in my deepest being. May your resurrection rise in me, Lord Christ. May it live in my very bones. Give me faith for this astonishing reality: because you overcame death, you can overcome anything.

Scripture says that your resurrection was "the first fruits"—the early part of the harvest. I ask for more harvest. More fruit where so far there has been little or none. More new life springing up where all seems dead and gone.

In your grace, bring your amazing resurrection power to my loved ones today, especially those who struggle with illness, disability, despair, and addiction.

Bring new life to my enemies. Bring new life to those who survive on the edges of society—to the homeless, the mentally ill, the forgotten elderly and incapacitated, the refugee, the incarcerated.

Rise, O living Lord, in all of us.

Amen.

‑¾ DAY 5

Blessed Are Those Who Mourn

Rejoice with those who rejoice, weep with those who weep.

ROMANS 12:15

With the promise of blessing in mourning, today's path is a prompt to hope in the power of redemption. The Beatitude isn't saying we should skip over pain and loss and just tell ourselves to be happy. Good mourning is healthy. We are allowing ourselves to do the honest, hard work of grief so that, in time, healing can occur. We position ourselves, too, to receive the Spirit's comfort. As the psalmist wrote, "The Lord is near to the brokenhearted" (Psalm 34:18).

| Stepping into the Path |
| Forgive Us Our Debts |
| Knowledge |
| Resurrection |
| Mourn |
| Be Comforted |

Loving Father,

Blessed are those who mourn.

You knew firsthand the meaning of mourning. You wept for dear friends. You suffered rejection, betrayal, and abandonment. You were saddened by the choices of people you loved—your family, your city, your nation.

So help us, your children, to find the blessing in mourning, and to believe in that blessing enough to wait for it.

Help us to give ourselves and others permission to mourn: for the loved ones we have lost, for the mistakes we have made, for the love we have failed to express. Give us the grace to celebrate with those who celebrate, and grieve with those who grieve.

Lift any who feel crushed by sorrow today, Lord. Heal our pain.

Thank you that there is no burden we could carry that you won't understand and carry with us.

Amen.

⚛ DAY 6

For They Will Be Comforted

Even though I walk through the darkest valley,
I fear no evil;
for you are with me;
your rod and your staff—
they comfort me.

PSALM 23:4

The second half of this Beatitude captures the essence of Jesus' message: Those who are hurting will receive comfort. Our pain will not last forever.

As you pray, ask God to help you see the outlines of hope in anything you suffer. "Weeping may linger for the night, but joy comes with the morning" (Psalm 30:5).

Stepping into
the Path

Forgive Us
Our Debts

Knowledge

Resurrection

Mourn

Be Comforted

Loving Comforter,

Today, I ask for comfort for all who need it.

Comfort those who are sick—people struggling with ongoing illness, or living in chronic pain.

Comfort the caregivers—those who give so much to others that they have nothing left.

Comfort the lonely—those who feel they have no support, no one who cares or understands.

Comfort the regretful—those who live in the shadow of guilt.

Comfort the fearful—the many plagued by threats both real and imagined.

Comfort those who wrestle with doubts—those diligent seekers to whom you feel distant and elusive.

Comfort all mourners—especially those whose hope for recovery is running out, whose bodies and minds are depleted.

You are the Spirit of Comfort. You bring the peace that passes understanding. Loving Comforter, renew all who grieve today. May your wonderful promise be lovingly fulfilled:

Blessed are those who mourn, for they will be comforted.

Amen.

Praying the Whole Path

By his great mercy he has given us a new birth into a living hope through the resurrection of Jesus Christ from the dead.

1 PETER 1:3

This week's path balances sorrow and joy. We sin and suffer loss, yes. That's part of life here on earth. But we can also ask for forgiveness and be set free from the debt of sin. In our mourning, we can receive the comfort of God; in a time of dying, we can cling to the promise of new life.

What debt of forgiveness can you release as you find your way home to God?

What for you might be "dead" that needs new life?

Where do you need to express mourning, that you may know the Spirit's comfort?

Stepping into the Path
Forgive Us Our Debts
Knowledge
Resurrection
Mourn
Be Comforted

Lord,

You know everything about me. Every thought and feeling and hope and fear play out before you, clear as day.

Help me always to ask you, boldly: forgive us our debts. You see my failings anyway, and you're not surprised by anything I do or think or feel. Help me to know that forgiveness is available, and that I can be as forgiving toward others as you are toward me.

Favor me with the gift of knowledge, that I would truly know your love, see your truth, and walk your path of life. By your Spirit, help me to live in the power of the resurrection, and to spread the good news of new life everywhere I go.

As I do, may I bring your comfort to all who need it. Make me a sensitive, welcome emissary of your promise: *blessed are those who mourn, for they will be comforted.* Make it true for me, that I may receive your comfort. And make it true for my life, as I announce and model your comfort for all those around me.

Thank you for this surprising path to new life.

Amen.

Connecting This Path with the Next

The connections between paths 5 and 6 are organic and rich with potential:

This week, we prayed for forgiveness. Next, we'll pray for daily support to keep us from straying again.

This week, we prayed to know what God wants us to know. Next, we'll pray to live what we know.

This week, we acknowledged the resurrection of Jesus. Next, we'll contemplate his ascension and his ongoing life in heaven.

WEEK 6

※

Lead Us Not into Temptation

✝

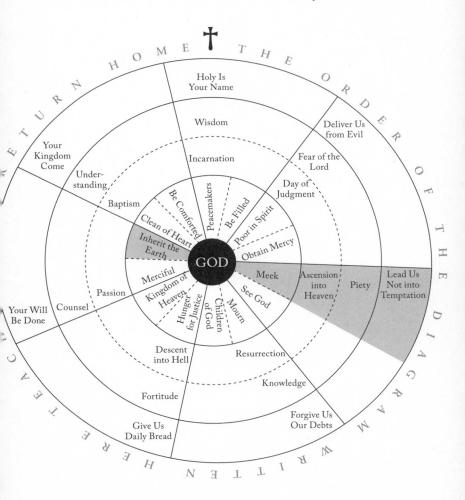

RETURN HOME · THE ORDER OF THE DIAGRAM WRITTEN HERE AS

- Holy Is Your Name
- Wisdom
- Incarnation
- Deliver Us from Evil
- Fear of the Lord
- Day of Judgment
- Your Kingdom Come
- Under-standing
- Baptism
- Be Comforted
- Peacemakers
- Be Filled
- Poor in Spirit
- Clean of Heart
- Inherit the Earth
- Obtain Mercy
- **GOD**
- Meek
- Ascension into Heaven
- Piety
- Lead Us Not into Temptation
- Merciful
- Kingdom of Heaven
- See God
- Passion
- Hunger for Justice
- Children of God
- Mourn
- Your Will Be Done
- Counsel
- Descent into Hell
- Resurrection
- Fortitude
- Knowledge
- Give Us Daily Bread
- Forgive Us Our Debts

Stepping into the Path

In all your ways acknowledge him,
and he will make straight your paths.

PROVERBS 3:6

Terms like "piety" or "meekness" are no longer heard much in some worship traditions. But this week's path shows how praying these terms can guide us to be more like Jesus.

Stepping into the Path
Lead Us Not into Temptation
Piety
Ascension into Heaven
Meek
Inherit the Earth

My father in heaven,

From you I come and to you one day I will return.

As I pray this week's path, help me to find my home in you.

◆

Lead us not into temptation.

◆

As I meditate on Christ's *ascension* into heaven, show me how the *gift of piety* can lead me in heaven's ways on earth.

◆

Blessed are the meek.

◆

For they will inherit the earth.

◆

You, O God, are my true home. Amen.

⤝ DAY 2

Lead Us Not into Temptation

God is faithful, and he will not let you be tested beyond
your strength, but with the testing he will also provide
the way out so that you may be able to endure it.

1 CORINTHIANS 10:13

In the last path, we prayed that God would forgive our sins.
Here we ask for help in avoiding new sin by praying to be spared
temptation—for protection from anyone or anything, including
ourselves, that might deceive us into sin.

Stepping into the Path
Lead Us Not into Temptation
Piety
Ascension into Heaven
Meek
Inherit the Earth

Loving God,

We confess today our tendency to wander, to fall back on the same old patterns even when they bring the same old harm.

May we find comfort in remembering that you were also tempted. You know what it's like to have the evil one parade before you all the glittering alternatives that lead to gloom in the end. You were faithful. Help us to be faithful, too.

May we find strength in knowing you are with us in our times of testing. Protect us, as you've promised. We will never not be human—please don't let us be tested beyond our ability to resist.

Throughout this day, draw us to you in mind and heart. May we thrive in the simple joy of your presence—listening for your leading, remembering your goodness, turning away again and again from exits to nowhere.

Thank you for your promise to show us the real way out—and help us to take it. When we are powerless, raise us up. Carry us to safety.

Amen.

⚛ DAY 3

Piety

Beware of practicing your piety before others in order to be seen by them; for then you have no reward from your Father in heaven.

MATTHEW 6:1

"Piety" has become a tarnished word in our day—it strikes us as a false, smarmy, or ostentatious show of faith. But in the classic sense, "piety" describes a humble and careful attention to God's presence and will. A pious person is God-minded without being showy about it.

Stepping into the Path
Lead Us Not into Temptation
Piety
Ascension into Heaven
Meek
Inherit the Earth

Heavenly Father,

Today, show me how to be God-minded without being self-righteous. How to wear my faith lightly, yet hold it deeply.

I want to find that way. I want to receive the gift of piety, that I may have a rich reservoir of faith and trust in you, without an ounce of self-regard seeping in.

Keep me holding fast to your ways, and let me not take pride in doing so.

May I be mindful of you first. May I look and listen for your will in all things.

Save me from making the gifts of spiritual practice—
    meditating,
    reading a sacred text,
    praying a sincere prayer,
    walking through the door of a church—
occasions for pride, for that warm feeling of achievement that I so easily mistake for your "well done."

Let piety be your work in me, your genuine goodness suffusing my heart.

In the meantime, thank you for receiving me . . . just as I am.

Amen.

Ascension into Heaven

But as it is, they desire a better country, that is, a heavenly one. Therefore God is not ashamed to be called their God; indeed he has prepared a city for them.

HEBREWS 11:16

Christ's return to heaven was not so much the end of his time on earth as it was the start of his eternal reign. Now, from heaven, the Bible says, Jesus continually advocates on our behalf. The wheel's pairing of piety with Christ's ascension might suggest that true devotion is an expression of God both in us and for us, divinity always drawing us toward itself.

Stepping into the Path
Lead Us Not into Temptation
Piety
Ascension into Heaven
Meek
Inherit the Earth

Lord Christ,

So often, we want to get out of here—out of this challenging world, out of our own heads. Some days, the idea of trading earth for heaven sounds irresistible.

Oh, to simply be with you! To be done with sorrow and strife. To have our problems erased, and our worries put behind us. Oh, to be forever at home in your presence!

You have made us from earth with an ache for heaven. And so many who have gone before us on this walk of faith also yearned for the day when they could see your face. Like them, we "desire a better country."

Yet remind us, Lord, that when you went back to heaven, your mission here was complete. Ours isn't yet. Teach us to take comfort in our ultimate destination without trying to escape your calling to the here and now.

Help us today to look ahead with joy. Help us to live in gratitude that you have already made a home for us in eternity with you.

Amen.

Blessed Are the Meek

And being found in human form,
he humbled himself
and became obedient to the point of death—
even death on a cross.

PHILIPPIANS 2:8

I n the Church's earliest years, Christians sang Philippians 2 as a hymn. It's significant that out of all the splendid themes they could have chosen—Christ's triumph over death, his glorious resurrection—they focused on his meekness, on what he gave up by becoming human and dying on a cross.

Stepping into the Path
Lead Us Not into Temptation
Piety
Ascension into Heaven
Meek
Inherit the Earth

Lord Jesus,

You have said that the meek are blessed, that those who choose to serve others for no personal gain will inherit the earth.

But how can this be, Lord? Please show us how. In our world, the meek get ignored. The humble end up trampled and left for dead.

Yet meekness is what you modeled. You gave up all privilege in order to become weak. You had divine power and prestige at your disposal, yet you chose to disguise God as a servant—even when that choice brought you suffering and death.

Show us today how to live with faith and confidence in your upside-down kingdom. Change our imagination, rearrange our priorities, re-create our very way of seeing. Otherwise, pride and power and winning make so much more sense.

Show us the giant promise of your "little" ways. Help us to desire humility, honor it in others, and choose it for ourselves, that we may do your true work and reveal your beauty in this world.

Amen.

For They Will Inherit the Earth

But the meek shall inherit the land,
and delight themselves in abundant prosperity.

PSALM 37:11

Jesus taught and demonstrated that in humility, there is strength. In meekness, he said, we inherit the earth. Meekness is how we live redemptively in the natural world.

To inherit the earth doesn't mean we seize it by force or have an unmitigated right to enter a forest with a chain saw. We don't inherit the earth by owning more property or consuming more resources. Following Christ's example, we approach our inheritance with meekness, receiving it as treasure to care for, as our Father intended.

Stepping into the Path
Lead Us Not into Temptation
Piety
Ascension into Heaven
Meek
Inherit the Earth

O Loving Creator,

Day by day unfolds in beauty.
    Your handiwork is magnificent.
    We praise you for the skies, for the fields, for the waters,
    for every creature that roams the earth.
    We are in awe of all that you have created.

Yet the planet reels under the assault of greed and indifference.
    We have not approached the earth in meekness.
    We have proudly exploited your world as if it were ours.
    So we pray for forgiveness; we pray for correction;
    we pray for a shared vision of how to make things right.

Turn our hearts again to you.
    As individuals, rich and poor;
    as communities; as corporations; as governments—
    make us humble in the face of your wonders.
    May we see earth, water, sky, and all living things
    as treasure on loan from you.
    We are your sons and daughters—may we find real abundance
    in thoughtful stewardship of your gifts.

Show us how to cherish our inheritance—
    for your honor and glory, and for the welfare of generations
    of heirs yet to be born.

Amen.

Praying the Whole Path

Humble yourselves before the Lord, and he will exalt you.

JAMES 4:10

Each day this week has invited us to feel the tension between heaven and earth. Devotion makes us long to be with Christ, yet we are called to a world of temptation and trial. For this space in between, the mysterious "blessing" of meekness arrives like a gift. Knowing that our lives are on loan—and not for self but for service—can help us become more fully present to his kingdom in the here and now, even as we look to heaven.

What are you tempted by?

How do you keep your mind on the things of heaven while attending fully to the things of earth?

Stepping into the Path
Lead Us Not into Temptation
Piety
Ascension into Heaven
Meek
Inherit the Earth

O most surprising Lord, teach me your ways:

You make what is not, so.

You ask me to trust utterly in what I can't see.

You teach me to pray "Keep me from temptation," but you ask me to follow you into the scuffle of the world—where your work is, and where I'm most likely to face trials and tests.

You show me that real strength comes often disguised as utter dependence.

You ascended to heaven, yet you still walk with us on earth.

You promise us the gift of piety; yet, to be honest, God, true devotion and false religiosity so often look the same to me.

You promise that those who give up the self—who choose meekness, who are meek—will get everything in the end.

O surprising Lord, today I open myself to you, whose ways I cannot comprehend.

Amen.

Connecting This Path with the Next

If the week just completed evoked the "path of heaven on earth," the seventh and final path tips the scales toward transcendence and eternity. We could describe it as "the path toward our eternal home." New Testament writers tended to frame earthly trials and persecutions as mere preparation for something glorious. As Paul prays in 1 Thessalonians, "May he so strengthen your hearts in holiness that you may be blameless before our God and Father at the coming of our Lord Jesus with all his saints."

WEEK 7

Deliver Us *from* Evil

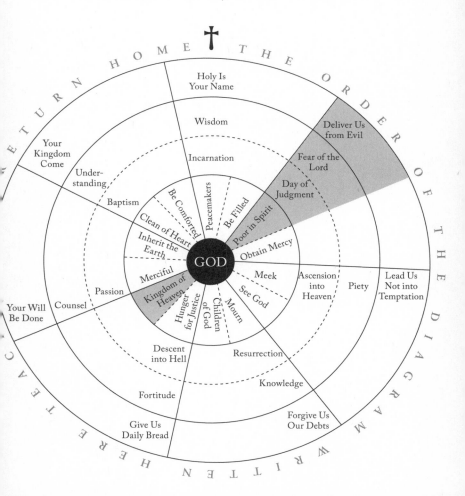

Stepping into the Path

You show me the path of life.

PSALM 16:11

This week's path invites us to pray through some dark words: Evil. Fear. Judgment. Poor. Yet glory shines through, too. Jesus makes his remarkable promise that the poor in spirit are especially blessed. And we are invited to consider how the daunting phrase "fear of the Lord" can open for us a life of surrender and awe.

Stepping into the Path
Deliver Us from Evil
Fear of the Lord
Day of Judgment
Poor in Spirit
Kingdom of Heaven

My father in heaven,

From you I come and to you one day I will return.

As I pray this week's path, help me to find my home in you.

◆

Deliver us from evil.

◆

As I consider the *Day of Judgment,* I open my being to receive the *gift of the fear of the Lord.*

◆

Blessed are the poor in spirit.

◆

For theirs is the kingdom of heaven.

◆

You, O God, are my true home. Amen.

Deliver Us from Evil

The Lord will rescue me from every evil attack and save me for his heavenly kingdom. To him be the glory forever and ever. Amen.

2 TIMOTHY 4:18

Some days are like this: You come home from sitting with your mother, who no longer recognizes you. Your daughter arrives home from school in tears, blurting out that her best friend called her a vile name. You watch the news and flinch: a terrorist attack abroad, a mass shooting here at home. Evil is all around.

The Lord's Prayer doesn't define "evil," but we already know what it looks and feels like. When we pray for deliverance, we are confessing our desperate need for God to save us from it.

Stepping into
the Path

Deliver Us
from Evil

Fear of
the Lord

Day of
Judgment

Poor in Spirit

Kingdom of
Heaven

All-Powerful Lord and Protector,

You are my loving Father, and I'm grateful that you want to protect me from harm. You are my strong defender. You are my rock of refuge.

Deliver me from evil:
    Grant me courage to stand firm in trials.
    Save me from my self-destructive impulses.
    Rescue me from fear, discouragement, and doubt.
    Shine your light where darkness threatens to overwhelm me.
    And graciously, by your Spirit, fill me with joy for the journey.

Deliver my family, community, and this world from evil:
    Grant us and our leaders the resolve to contend for the right.
    Save us from violence, hatred, war, and oppression.
    Rescue us from acting out of fear, anger, or prejudice.
    Shine your light wherever darkness threatens to overwhelm.
    And graciously, by your Spirit, renew us and our world in your unfailing love.

Amen.

Fear of the Lord

My thoughts are not your thoughts,
nor are your ways my ways, says the Lord.
For as the heavens are higher than the earth,
so are my ways higher than your ways
and my thoughts than your thoughts.

ISAIAH 55:8–9

Like the words "piety" and "meekness," the phrase "fear of the Lord" may need updating for contemporary seekers. The Father doesn't want to scare us into believing in his love. This "fear" begins in an awareness of God's total otherness, found in the unimaginable expanse of the universe or the majesty of the sea. As God spoke to the prophet Isaiah: "My thoughts are not your thoughts, nor are your ways my ways."

Seen in this light, the gift of holy fear leads us to fall on our knees in worship. We are struck dumb—not by dread, but by amazement.

Stepping into
the Path

Deliver Us
from Evil

Fear of
the Lord

Day of
Judgment

Poor in Spirit

Kingdom of
Heaven

Holy Father,

Sometimes I am afraid of you,
    or at least of my idea of you—
        afraid of being exposed; afraid of being punished.
        But this fear pushes me away from you,
        whose nearness is my good.

Open my eyes to who you really are, to what
    a Spirit-born fear is supposed to elicit in my life.

Dismantle my small, self-centered, convenient ideas about you.
    Replace the illusions with glimpses of your true glory.
    Bring forth my deepest reverence.
    Build in me a lifestyle of praise.

You, Lord, are like an ocean—too deep to fathom,
    too wonderful to comprehend.
        You are greater than all matter, all energy, all time.
        Your very name is the essence of mystery and might.

Today I ask you to grace me with an abiding, life-shaping fear of
you. By your Spirit, reveal your divine nature so I can
    trust you more fully,
    seek your best with my whole heart, and
    serve you with joy.

Amen.

Day of Judgment

He judges the world with righteousness;
he judges the peoples with equity.

PSALM 9:8

Judgment is something that most of us would like to postpone, perhaps indefinitely. But consider: a coming day of reckoning—of making all things right—frees us from the compulsion to judge. Judging ourselves or others is not our business; God has that one covered.

Also, the prospect of an eternal settling of accounts gives us the hope that, even in our darkest times, every overlooked effort we make for good will count for something in the long run. We don't need to wonder what it's all for: God has already told us that it's for his kingdom.

Stepping into
the Path

Deliver Us
from Evil

Fear of
the Lord

Day of
Judgment

Poor in Spirit

Kingdom of
Heaven

Merciful God,

When I think of the pain and suffering in this world,
    I know your judgment cannot come too soon.
    The unprincipled do great evil against the vulnerable.
    The poor are at every disadvantage, while the rich and proud
    grow in strength, opportunity, and power.

When will this change? How long, O Lord,
    until you make things right?
    Life is so unfair!
    When will your day of justice come?
    When will you set the captives free once and for all?

Merciful God, open my eyes more and more every day,
    to who you are, and to what you want.
    And, Lord Jesus Christ, son of God, when you come
    to make all things right, have mercy on me, a sinner.
    Cover me with your righteousness.

Help me to look to that day—
    not with dread, or resistance, or running away from you—
    but with longing and hope
    for myself, and for all who suffer,
    and for every living creature.

Amen.

⚹ DAY 5

Blessed Are the Poor in Spirit

The Lord is near to the brokenhearted,
and saves the crushed in spirit.

PSALM 34:18

Even though it occurs last in our wheel, this Beatitude is the one that Jesus utters first. In Matthew's gospel, Jesus blesses those who are "poor in spirit" (Matthew 5:3). In Luke's gospel, Jesus says simply, "Blessed are the poor" (Luke 6:20). Both physical and emotional poverty are closely linked.

The Greek language had a couple of different words to describe a person as poor. The first one referred to what we'd call the working poor—folks who earned a subsistence living but had no luxuries. The second described complete destitution and utter dependence. At its root, that word meant to "cower" or to "cringe away." That second word is the one Jesus chose to use here.

In Jesus' time, and for many today, abject poverty of this sort was considered a curse. Yet Jesus upheld it as blessed.

Stepping into the Path
Deliver Us from Evil
Fear of the Lord
Day of Judgment
Poor in Spirit
Kingdom of Heaven

Heavenly Father,

Bless those living in poverty today.

Pour out heaven's best on all those who are without food, shelter, clothing, jobs, and every other kind of support. Awaken all those with means to care for the poor to come to their aid.

Sometimes the impoverished one is me.
Sometimes the one called to provide is me.

May you also bless those who are poor in spirit today, as you have promised.

Pour out heaven's best on all those who feel stripped of hope and respect, and weighed down by anxiety or hopelessness. Awaken all those with means to care for the poor in spirit to come to their aid.

Sometimes the impoverished one is me.
Sometimes the one called to provide is me.

Thank you for your astonishing promise that those who have nothing inside or out already possess everything that endures.

Amen.

⁕ DAY 6

Theirs Is the Kingdom of Heaven

But strive first for the kingdom of God and his righteousness,
and all these things will be given to you as well.

MATTHEW 6:33

J esus' kingdom is—and will be—filled with those who are now outcasts. No earthly kingdom is that way now, nor ever has been. Yet this extraordinary truth undergirds every point of the message of Jesus: God aims to turn things around. The hurting will stop hurting. The sick will be well. The materially and spiritually poor will inherit the most prosperous kingdom the universe will ever know.

Stepping into the Path
Deliver Us from Evil
Fear of the Lord
Day of Judgment
Poor in Spirit
Kingdom of Heaven

Lord,

Your kingdom is so different from what's valued in my world.

We worship riches and fame and power, and flashy shows of strength, but you say those advantages have no value in your kingdom. You came as a servant, and call us to serve and honor others. You say that in our weakness, your power shines through.

We prize physical beauty, but the beauty that matters to you comes from inside. It shows up best in acts of kindness, in living with courage, integrity, and humility.

We praise the self. We live as though the universe revolves around our wants and needs, our potential, our success. But you came to radically change our worldview. You showed us how to honor our humanity and find our freedom in you.

Renew my vision of your kingdom, Lord, and help me to seek it every day. Make my vision clear. Teach me to care for the things of God and the ways of God over everything that's valued in the kingdom of this world.

Amen.

Praying the Whole Path

Do not be wise in your own eyes;
fear the Lord, and turn away from evil.

PROVERBS 3:7

L ike a lot of the wheel, this path retrains our brains, inviting us to become comfortable with the counterintuitive but enduring realities of Jesus' gospel.

What's the most challenging step for you in this path?

Which step makes you hungry for more growth?

Stepping into the Path
Deliver Us from Evil
Fear of the Lord
Day of Judgment
Poor in Spirit
Kingdom of Heaven

Loving God,

You are my true home, the source of my identity and value, my only unassailable place of safety, comfort, and rest.

Help me to always return home. Whenever I stray or forget, help me to hear you calling me back.

In returning to you, I ask you to *deliver me from evil*.

In returning to you, I want to learn to humbly *fear* you.

In returning to you, I ask you to show me the true wealth of the *poor in spirit*.

In returning to you, I trust fully in your good *judgment*—your promise to put all things right in me and in my world.

May what is true for me be true for all of your creation. May the *kingdom of heaven* come, as you bring healing, peace, and renewal to the whole world.

Amen.

Connecting This Path with the Next

The seventh path in the wheel leads us back to the first one, and invites us to pray the paths again in a continual experience of learning and devotion.

For example, fear of the Lord, the gift of the seventh path, comes right before the gift of wisdom, the gift of the first path. Proverbs 9:10 points to the link between deep reverence and wisdom: "The fear of the Lord is the beginning of wisdom."

PART 2

Praying the Wheel for Everyday Life

*From there you will seek the Lord your God, and you will find
him if you search after him with all your heart and soul.*

DEUTERONOMY 4:29

This part models nine topical journeys that show how praying
through the wheel can help you bring the message of Jesus and
the gifts of the Spirit to specific needs, or can help you in doing
intercessory prayer on behalf of people you love.

For each topic here, we have chosen a petition, a relevant gift, an
event from Christ's life, and a Beatitude. The left-hand page gives
you a scripture text plus a visual guide to the corresponding parts
of the wheel. On the right, we suggest a prayer inspired by them.

You may still find it helpful to manually trace your prayer around
the wheel. Doing this will not only help you not lose your place but
also ground you physically in the rich sequences and proximities of
this ancient guide.

⚜ TO EXPRESS GRATITUDE

*One of his disciples, Andrew, Simon Peter's brother, said
to him, "There is a boy here who has five barley loaves and
two fish. But what are they among so many people?"*

*Jesus said, "Make the people sit down." Now there was a great deal of
grass in the place; so they sat down, about five thousand in all. Then
Jesus took the loaves, and when he had given thanks, he distributed
them to those who were seated; so also the fish, as much as they wanted.*

JOHN 6:8–11

This story from the Gospel of John takes place just before the
start of the Passover festival, a detail that
turns out to be important to understanding
what Jesus is trying to do. In the Old Testament, the Passover marked the beginning of
God's liberation of his people. Throughout the
forty years that followed, God miraculously
provided daily bread (in the form of manna)
from heaven.

Here, the gospel gives us another story of
God providing bread for his people, seemingly
out of nowhere. And these provisions still happen for us today, if we have the eyes to see.

Petition: Give us this day our daily bread.

Gift: Fear of the Lord

Event: Ascension into Heaven

Beatitude: Blessed are the poor in spirit, for theirs is the kingdom of heaven.

O Lord Christ,

Your generosity is unfailing and extravagant. Thank you! We worry and fret that we won't have enough, but you care for us. Provider, Source, Giver—these are your very names. You give us *our daily bread* and so much more. You grant us your comfort, your compassion and strength, your abiding Spirit.

We are deeply grateful for all your gifts!

The *fear of the Lord* is a gift, too—a nudge to love and revere you, all-powerful God; a reminder that our lives are meant to be about more than ourselves; an internal prompt in the midst of all our preoccupations to embrace humility.

You broke bread with us on earth, but you are more than earth. Since your *ascension* from this planet, you have lived and reigned in your heavenly kingdom, where you will welcome us home one day. Thank you!

Do *the poor in spirit* really inherit the *kingdom of heaven*? You promised, and in faith we accept it as true. And may heaven arrive through us today as we share your love and hope with others.

Like those hungry followers on the hillside that day, we look to you for what only you can provide. And you do. For this, we give you our thanks and praise.

Amen.

⫶ IN TIMES OF GRIEF

Even though I walk through the darkest valley,
I fear no evil;
for you are with me;
your rod and your staff—
they comfort me.

PSALM 23:4

N o one wants to go through grief and loss, yet these trials can bring us closer to God. Jesus promised that when we mourn, we will be comforted. In this prayer, we find comfort in the timeless truths of the Christian story: that God became human and felt our pain, that we can have knowledge of God's deeds and love for us, and that God's kingdom is already under way.
In our grief, we can cling to those truths and fear no evil, for God is with us.

Petition: Your kingdom come.

Gift:
Knowledge

Event:
Incarnation

Beatitude:
Blessed are those who mourn, for they shall be comforted.

Loving Shepherd,

I cry out to you from the depths of loss. I can't stop thinking about everything I used to have, the love I used to know. It's painful to remember how blessed I was when my loved ones were around me—just as it's painful to admit that I didn't always appreciate everything I had at the time.

Why, Lord? Why do we love, and then lose the ones we love? Why did you allow death into the world that you called "good"?

May your kingdom come, Lord—your promised reordering of reality, where you will wipe away every tear, and death will have no more sting. Every other kingdom is only temporary.

Grant me insights from your Spirit today that I wouldn't have otherwise. Bless me with the *gift of knowledge,* so that I can see your hand in all things and know, even in this dark season, that your promises are true. You will never abandon me. Like a shepherd, you are leading me through this valley of shadows.

In my great need, I cling to the miracle of your *incarnation.* You took on human flesh and every messy, aching feeling that went with it—including suffering and loss. When you lost your friend Lazarus, you cried bitter tears.

Today, help me to reach for your promise that, as one of those who *mourn, I will be comforted.* Help me to look for and receive that comfort. Thank you that you are walking with me, even here, even now.

Amen.

⚘ HELP WITH A DECISION

And when you turn to the right or when you turn to the left, your ears shall hear a word behind you, saying, "This is the way; walk in it."

ISAIAH 30:21

Wouldn't it be great if, every time we faced an important decision, God would deliver our directions turn by turn out loud? Spiritual discernment doesn't quite work that way. But when we pray for understanding, then listen for God's will, we do become more adept at sensing that "still, small voice" leading us on the path ahead.

Petition: Your will be done.

Gift: Understanding

Event: Day of Judgment

Beatitude: Blessed are the meek, for they shall inherit the earth.

God,

I'm at a crossroads, and I need your guidance to show me which way to choose. And I sincerely want *your will done* in my life. That's everything to me, Lord. But I struggle to see how that should happen, especially as I face the decision ahead.

Help me choose well. I want to be glad about my choices, so that as my life unfolds, I have no regrets, and so that when I stand in your presence on that great *Day of Judgment*, I will hear your "well done."

That's why I'm so grateful today for your Holy Spirit. You promise to give *understanding*—insights that are not my own; an inner reassurance when I'm doing the right thing.

Thank you for showing me what I can't see. You know where your kingdom is at work.

And thank you that in this life, I don't have to make perfect choices. Thank you that you can work in all things, if I let you.

Help me to listen for your leading even when I'm sure I know the way. But you said, *Blessed are the meek*. So I simply ask for the grace of meekness.

Show me your ways in spite of myself.

I love you, God. At this and every crossroads in my life, may your will be done.

Amen.

⚹ IN TIMES OF JOY

*Although you have not seen him, you love him; and even
though you do not see him now, you believe in him and rejoice
with an indescribable and glorious joy, for you are receiving
the outcome of your faith, the salvation of your souls.*

1 PETER 1:8–9

In Christian worship services around the world, you're likely to
hear the congregation exclaim, "God is good—all the time!"
Somehow this simple statement captures the joy we feel in God's
presence. When our hearts bubble up with gratitude for answers to
prayer, for our new life in Christ, or for the promise of the resurrection, we respond with praise, and with spreading the good news.
God is good . . . all the time!

> *Petition:* Holy
> is your name.
>
> *Gift:*
> Piety
>
> *Event:*
> Resurrection
>
> *Beatitude:*
> Blessed are the
> peacemakers,
> for they shall be
> called children
> of God.

Father,

Your name is holy! You are perfection—the very source of joy!

That's why I come to you with thanksgiving and praise today. And something like real joy. Thank you. My life isn't perfect, but you are good, and everything you do is good.

To me, your name is another word for everything good!

I thank you for your ongoing work of *piety* in my heart. May you continue to shape my thoughts and actions by the joy, praise, and reverence I feel right at this moment. More and more, may your mind renew my mind.

To me—I'll just say it, God—your name stands for everything beautiful!

I am so grateful for the promise of *resurrection*. Jesus rose from the dead, defeating death and sin for all time. Because he overcame death, we can, too. We are mortal, but you have made us for eternity.

To me, your name is the very promise of life!

Help me today to put joy into action by *being your peacemaker,* bringing serenity, hope, justice, and reconciliation to others.

Amen.

⚼ FOR FORGIVENESS

When they kept on questioning him, he straightened up and said to them, "Let anyone among you who is without sin be the first to throw a stone at her." And once again he bent down and wrote on the ground.

When they heard it, they went away, one by one, beginning with the elders; and Jesus was left alone with the woman standing before him. Jesus straightened up and said to her, "Woman, where are they? Has no one condemned you?" She said, "No one, sir." And Jesus said, "Neither do I condemn you. Go your way, and from now on do not sin again."

JOHN 8:7–11

The Bible says that all of us have sinned and fallen short of the glory of God. When that happens, the Spirit nudges us to turn around and get back on the right path. This prayer draws on parts of the wheel that encourage us to reflect on where we've strayed and to ask for forgiveness, knowing that God is merciful, and his love unfailing.

Petition:
Forgive us our debts.

Gift:
Fear of the Lord

Event:
Passion

Beatitude:
Blessed are the clean of heart, for they shall see God.

Lord Jesus,

When good people were ready to stone a woman who had sinned, you stepped in to remind them that they were all sinners, too.

That's also me you were talking about. I'm a sinner. Like that woman, sometimes I feel too ashamed to expect anything but judgment.

Forgive me my debts, Lord—all the uncountable ways I have hurt others, hurt myself, and betrayed you. And bless me with the gift of the *fear of the Lord,* that I may always place you first in my life.

Remind me through the story of your *passion* that you carried all my sins, all my sorrow and suffering. You've already paid the price. Thank you, gracious Lord.

Make me *clean* all through right now, so that I can know and share your mercy more truly. I want to be like the woman who left your presence free and forgiven, and feeling deeply, unconditionally loved by you.

Amen.

⚘ FOR CALM

And when he got into the boat, his disciples followed him.
A windstorm arose on the sea, so great that the boat was
being swamped by the waves; but he was asleep.

And they went and woke him up, saying, "Lord, save us! We are
perishing!" And he said to them, "Why are you afraid, you of little
faith?" Then he got up and rebuked the winds and the sea; and
there was a dead calm. They were amazed, saying, "What sort
of man is this, that even the winds and the sea obey him?"

MATTHEW 8:23–27

Some days we can feel like we are drowning in anxiety. This may reflect major worries, like injustice or poor health, or it may come from an accumulation of irritations that, taken individually, don't amount to much. Either experience can cause us to cry out, "Lord, save us! We are perishing!" This prayer for calm reminds us that God has the power to show his care and bring peace in any storm.

Petition:
Your will
be done.

Gift:
Wisdom

Event:
Baptism

Beatitude:
Blessed are the
peacemakers,
for they shall be
called children
of God.

Jesus,

Today, I cry out with the disciples, "Lord, save me!" I feel caught in a storm at sea, and it's all I can do to stay in the boat.

In the midst of the tumult, may *your will be done* in my life *as it is in heaven*. You are the Lord of peace. Bring peace here. Help me to see past my fear to your calming presence. You have this under control, even if your timing and will are not apparent to me.

Grant me the gift of *wisdom* in this turmoil to see where your Spirit is already at work for my deliverance. Broaden my perspective today; give me insight into what things look like from your point of view.

You know me by name. At my *baptism*, I was marked and sealed as your precious child. You claimed me as your own, placing me under your protection. I hold tightly to that promise now, to the settled confidence that I belong to you.

I know that when you said *Blessed are the peacemakers,* you were calling your followers to be reconciled to you, to each other, and to ourselves. Right now I lay my anxieties down, Lord Jesus, so that your peace can replace them in my heart. Show me how I can bring your peace to others.

Amen.

⚵ FOR HOPE IN HARD TIMES

*For surely I know the plans I have for you, says the Lord, plans
for your welfare and not for harm, to give you a future with hope.
Then when you call upon me and come and pray to me, I will hear
you. When you search for me, you will find me; if you seek me
with all your heart, I will let you find me, says the Lord, and I
will restore your fortunes and gather you from all the nations and
all the places where I have driven you, says the Lord, and I will
bring you back to the place from which I sent you into exile.*

JEREMIAH 29:11–14

Some trials are so intense and long, they can best be described
as a kind of living hell. This promise from God came through
Jeremiah, a prophet who ministered during
years of nearly unrelieved fear, trauma, and
death. Trials of any kind make the truths of
this prayer precious. But especially when evil
seems to prevail, we treasure the promise that
God will bring us "a future with hope."

Petition:
Deliver us
from evil.

Gift:
Counsel

Event:
Descent into
Hell

Beatitude:
Blessed are the
merciful, for
they shall
obtain mercy.

Great Deliverer,

I never really thought I'd be here, sunk so low. Right now it's hard to remember a time when I felt happy. Please hear my cry!

Deliver me from evil, Lord. I feel hopeless. Shine your light in my heart today. Restore my hope in you, and my faith in your good purposes for me.

Through your gift of *counsel,* help me discern where your Spirit is already working. Like the first crocuses peeking out of the cold, hard ground in early spring, there are signs all around me that your Spirit is bringing life from darkness. Open my eyes to see it today, I pray.

When you *descended into hell,* you showed that nothing is beyond your power and grace. You overcame the worst so that we could know the best—life, goodness, and, yes, happiness.

And *be merciful* unto me, Lord, as I am *merciful.* Help me not lash out in pain. Instead, transform my pit of suffering into a wellspring of compassion and grace that I can bring to others.

You are a God who delivers. You are a God who blesses. Thank you. But, oh, hear my cry today! Graciously and generously, deliver me from despair and restore me to hope.

Amen.

⚹ FOR HEALING FROM ILLNESS

Are any among you sick? They should call for the elders of the church and have them pray over them, anointing them with oil in the name of the Lord. The prayer of faith will save the sick, and the Lord will raise them up; and anyone who has committed sins will be forgiven.

JAMES 5:14–15

I n the New Testament, the words for "healing" and "saving" are one and the same, which points to something important about the Christian life. While we focus on a physical recovery, we know that God's healing touch may be more spiritual in nature. Today we pray for the fortitude of healing, and also for the fortitude to endure.

Petition:
Give us this day
our daily bread.

Gift:
Fortitude

Event:
Incarnation

Beatitude:
Blessed are the
poor in spirit,
for theirs is the
kingdom of
heaven.

God of healing,

In my sickness this day, this hour, I ask for the physical, spiritual, and emotional nourishment I need to get me through. Grant me an infusion of health and recovery. You know exactly what I need—*give me daily bread.*

By your touch, revive my heart and my body in this time of sickness. Grant me your gift of *fortitude.* I ask you to heal me, if that is your will. And in the meantime, help me endure my circumstances with humility and courage. Strengthen me through sleepless nights and dragging days.

When you became *incarnate,* you took on the miseries of human experience for yourself. That must have included illness and disease. You made yourself weak on purpose—what an amazing act of grace! Thank you that you understand.

Remind me, when I feel powerless, that the *poor in spirit* are actually in a blessed state. In my time of great need, something about your *kingdom of heaven* is nearer than ever—perhaps is already mine. Please show it to me.

Surround me with the prayers of the faithful today, loving God. Anoint me with the riches that can be inherited only when I feel my great need.

I love and trust you, O God who heals.

Amen.

⚜ TO PRAISE GOD

Bless the Lord, O my soul,
*   and all that is within me,*
*   bless his holy name.*
Bless the Lord, O my soul,
*   and do not forget all his benefits—*
who forgives all your iniquity,
*   who heals all your diseases,*
who redeems you from life in the Pit,
*   who crowns you with steadfast love and mercy,*
who satisfies you with good as long as you live
*   so that your youth is renewed like the eagle's.*

PSALM 103:1–5

The wheel leads us in many ways to praise God for his abundant gifts to us in this life. The psalm quoted here starts with a jubilant call to the individual—to body, mind, heart, and soul—to "not forget" God's lavish blessings. In today's prayer, enlightened by the gift of knowledge, we remember and enumerate some of them.

Petition:
Holy is
your name.

Gift:
Knowledge

Event:
Ascension into
Heaven

Beatitude:
Blessed are the
meek, for they
shall inherit the
earth.

I bless you, Lord, with every part of my being!

I honor *your name as holy* in all of heaven and earth. Your name is beautiful to my ears and to my lips. It is a joy to be able to speak your name to the skies.

I'm grateful for *knowledge* of you and what you've done to love and protect me. I will not forget your benefits to me. You are worthy of all my praise and worship forever!

I praise you, *ascended* Christ, who reigns with love and justice over all creation. You brought the words of life. You *are* life. You are greater than any power in the universe. Yet you love me with unfailing kindness. Thank you!

I live for your promise that the *meek will be blessed, for they shall inherit the earth.* Hallelujah! No heart is too lowly for your Spirit to enter, Lord. When I humble myself, I can see your wonders more clearly.

You have forgiven me, redeemed me, rescued me, and crowned me for a lifetime of your steadfast mercy and love.

I do not forget—oh, help me not to forget! With everything in me today, I bless you, Lord.

Amen.

⚷ PRAYING THE WHEEL FOR OTHERS

I pray that, according to the riches of his glory, he may grant that you may be strengthened in your inner being with power through his Spirit, and that Christ may dwell in your hearts through faith, as you are being rooted and grounded in love. I pray that you may have the power to comprehend, with all the saints, what is the breadth and length and height and depth, and to know the love of Christ that surpasses knowledge, so that you may be filled with all the fullness of God.

EPHESIANS 3:16–19

Some of the most treasured prayers in the New Testament are intercessory ones: petitions a person makes on another's behalf. Jesus' prayer for his disciples, as recorded in John 17, is a notable example. Paul often included impassioned prayers in his letters to the churches. In the one quoted here, you can almost trace the relevant texts from the wheel.

Petition:
Lead [name of person] not into temptation.

Gift:
Wisdom

Event:
Ascension into Heaven

Beatitude:
Blessed are those who hunger for justice, for they shall be filled.

Heavenly Father,

I come before you today with [names] on my mind. Let them know your love above all things.

Lead [names] not into temptation, and don't let them be tested beyond what they can handle. Instead may they be strengthened in body and soul so they can resist lesser preoccupations and harmful distractions.

Because Christ *ascended into heaven* and promised to send the Spirit in his place, I can ask with confidence that you will touch them with your Spirit. Fill them with a clear sense that Christ is alive in their heart.

Help [names] grow in the gift of *wisdom*, able to evaluate problems, questions, and relationships with the kind of insight only you can give. Nurture them so they grow deep in your love, completely prepared to do great things for you in this world.

Teach them always to *hunger for your justice*, that they may be blessed, and that through them, your best would come to others. Each day, reveal to them more of you—whose goodness and love are measureless and free.

Amen.

PART 3

Praying the Scriptures with the Wheel

Your word is a lamp to my feet
and a light to my path.

PSALM 119:105

Christians have prayed with scripture from the earliest days of the faith. Indeed, the first time we see the early Church praying (Acts 4), they are reciting Psalm 2. That's especially fitting, since Psalms is a prayer book, but prayers appear throughout the Bible, and Christians have long recited the prayers that were first uttered by biblical figures: Moses, Sarah, Hannah, Mary, and so on.

All sorts of scriptures can be incorporated into prayer, and from the monastics forward, certain approaches have come into widespread use.

One is called *lectio divina,* a Benedictine practice where slow, meditative reading turns into prayer. *Lectio divina* means "divine reading," and it's meant to prompt you to read scripture differently than normal. *Lectio* happens in four stages:

- First, you select a brief passage and *read* it slowly, carefully.

- Second, you *reflect* on it, spend time with it, turn it over in your mind.

- Third, you *respond* to it prayerfully, letting your heart speak to God.

- Fourth, you *rest* in the passage, listening contemplatively for what God might reveal to you.

Read, reflect, respond, and rest/contemplate. *Lectio divina* began as a communal practice, but it can be done individually as well.

Another practice is known as *gospel contemplation*, taught by Saint Ignatius of Loyola in the sixteenth century. Here, you focus on one gospel passage, often one where Jesus is mixing with other people. As with *lectio*, you read the passage slowly, preferably multiple times. Then you imagine your way into the story as closely and carefully as you can, before asking: Who am I in this scene? What is Jesus saying to me? How am I responding?

Here in Part 3, we're inspired by *lectio divina* and gospel contemplation. The basic idea is to use scripture to go deeper with the wheel, and use the wheel to go deeper with scripture—all with the intention of enriching the prayer experience.

What follows is a week's worth of scriptures suggested by the wheel. For each day, one part of the wheel—a word, a section, or a path—is paired with a passage of scripture. You'll find a brief introduction to the passage, and a prompt to read it for yourself. Then you'll find a written prayer you can use as your own, or as inspiration for your own conversation with God.

For the most part, these prayers are keyed to whole Bible chapters or large sections of chapters rather than to individual verses.

As you read the verses, you may want to read passages surrounding these selections to get even more scriptural context.

To get started praying scriptures with the wheel, we offer a fitting invocation. In 1549, Thomas Cranmer published these beautiful words in the first edition of the Anglican Book of Common Prayer:

> *Blessed Lord, who hast caused all holy Scriptures to be written for our learning: Grant us that we may in such wise hear them, read, mark, learn, and inwardly digest them; that, by patience and comfort of thy holy Word, we may embrace and ever hold fast the blessed hope of everlasting life, which thou hast given us in our Savior Jesus Christ.*

Happy Is the One Who Listens to Wisdom

Proverbs 8

In Proverbs 8, and continuing through chapter 9, we meet a woman who personifies wisdom, and speaks with great urgency to anyone who will listen. Lady Wisdom, as she's often called, is pictured standing at the gates of a city, calling out to passersby. "Listen to me! Receive wisdom, and everything else will follow!" she says in essence. "If you want to be blessed, choose wisdom! That's the only way to have what you need to succeed in life, to manage your day, to be who and what you need to be!"

As if by divine arrangement, all the spiritual gifts we have encountered in the Prayer Wheel—understanding, counsel, fortitude, knowledge, piety, and the fear of the Lord—are here. The term "piety" does not appear literally, but it is clearly conveyed by "the way of righteousness," and by the picture of Wisdom "rejoicing always in [the Lord's] presence."

Read the passage thoughtfully. If you have time, read it again, allowing the scenes and admonitions to fuse in your imagination. When you're ready, let the prayer on page 155 be yours, or use it as inspiration for your own Proverbs 8 prayer.

✳

1   Does not wisdom call,
     and does not understanding raise her voice?
2   On the heights, beside the way,
     at the crossroads she takes her stand;
3   beside the gates in front of the town,
     at the entrance of the portals she cries out:
4   "To you, O people, I call,
     and my cry is to all that live.
5   O simple ones, learn prudence;
     acquire intelligence, you who lack it.
6   Hear, for I will speak noble things,
     and from my lips will come what is right. . . .
8   All the words of my mouth are righteous,
     there is nothing twisted or crooked in them. . . .

10   Take my instruction instead of silver,
     and knowledge rather than choice gold;
11   for wisdom is better than jewels,
     and all that you may desire cannot compare with her.
12   I, wisdom, live with prudence,
     and I attain knowledge and discretion. . . .

20   I walk in the way of righteousness,
     along the paths of justice,
21   endowing with wealth those who love me,
     and filling their treasuries. . . .

33   Hear instruction and be wise,
      and do not neglect it.
34   Happy is the one who listens to me,
      watching daily at my gates,
      waiting beside my doors.
35   For whoever finds me finds life
      and obtains favor from the Lord;
36   but those who miss me injure themselves;
      all who hate me love death."

Lord God,

Your word says, *Does not wisdom call, and does not understanding raise her voice?* (v. 1).

Yes, God—creation itself reflects your nature. Every cell and atom reveals order, value, and meaning. Yet, all around I see the consequences of foolish choices. As I go through my day, give me ears to hear wisdom calling out to be heard.

All the words of wisdom are righteous; there is nothing twisted or crooked in them. . . . All that you may desire cannot compare with her (vv. 8, 11).

Help me to choose living wisely over any other kind of living. When other options look more appealing or popular, strengthen me to choose integrity, self-discipline, and common sense.

I walk in the way of righteousness, along the paths of justice (v. 20).

Keep me on time-tested paths, Lord. For decisions I face today, help me not to act until I've listened carefully for what wisdom is trying to tell me. If it takes me a while to figure things out, grant me patience, humility, and persistence. Then grant me the strength to do what's right for myself and others. For you have said,

Happy is the one who listens to me [wisdom],
    watching daily at my gates. . . .
For whoever finds me finds life
    and obtains favor from the Lord (vv. 34–35).

Amen.

A Celebration of Freedom

Romans 8

The Prayer Wheel path that begins "Forgive Us Our Debts" fits Romans 8 like a hand into a glove. It's all here: forgiveness of sins, knowledge of Christ, resurrection of our bodies, and comfort.

This chapter is the culmination of an argument Paul has been building throughout this letter, his longest. Many consider the Letter to the Romans to be Paul's magnum opus because it deals with so many of the biggest theological questions: Why are we separated from God? What has God done to bring us back to him? How are we supposed to respond to what God has done? How can we know that we've responded, and that we've really returned to God?

Read Romans 8—once or twice, and preferably aloud. Then look over the Forgive Us Our Debts path on the Prayer Wheel. Once you've compared the two, you'll be ready to offer your own prayer, or follow the prayer we suggest on page 159.

1   There is therefore now no condemnation for those who are in Christ Jesus. 2 For the law of the Spirit of life in Christ Jesus has set you free from the law of sin and of death. 3 For God has done what the law, weakened by the flesh, could not do: by sending his own Son in the likeness of sinful flesh, and to deal with sin, he condemned sin in the flesh, 4 so that the just requirement of the law might be fulfilled in us, who walk not according to the flesh but according to the Spirit. . . .

11 If the Spirit of him who raised Jesus from the dead dwells in you, he who raised Christ from the dead will give life to your mortal bodies also through his Spirit that dwells in you. . . .

13 If you live according to the flesh, you will die; but if by the Spirit you put to death the deeds of the body, you will live. 14 For all who are led by the Spirit of God are children of God. 15 For you did not receive a spirit of slavery to fall back into fear, but you have received a spirit of adoption. When we cry, "Abba! Father!" 16 it is that very Spirit bearing witness with our spirit that we are children of God, 17 and if children, then heirs. . . .

28 We know that all things work together for good for those who love God, who are called according to his purpose. . . .

31   If God is for us, who is against us? 32 He who did not withhold his own Son, but gave him up for all of us, will he not with him also give us everything else? . . . 35 Who will separate us from the love of Christ? Will hardship, or distress, or persecution, or famine, or nakedness, or peril, or sword? . . .

37   No, in all these things we are more than conquerors through him who loved us. 38 For I am convinced that neither death, nor life, nor angels, nor rulers, nor things present, nor things to come, nor powers, 39 nor height, nor depth, nor anything else in all creation, will be able to separate us from the love of God in Christ Jesus our Lord.

Compassionate Father,

Forgiveness is the white robe you wrap me in. Grace is your first order of business.

When, like the prodigal son, I turn from my rebellion and head for home, you accept me as I am. There's nothing about me that you condemn or reject—nothing at all (v. 1).

You want me to live a free and full life, a life whose source is your Spirit (vv. 3–4).

The same Spirit that raised Jesus from the dead raises me to new life every day. You help me put an end to the things that drag me down. In you, I am being made new (vv. 11, 13)!

You have adopted me as your own child, one of your heirs (vv. 14–17).

You are working everything out for me. Just like a good father, you're taking care of your children, setting me up, leading me on, showing me the way (v. 28).

If you are for me, who can be against me? Who can condemn me, when you are bringing me to life? Even when I fall, you declare that, in the end, I'll be victorious. Nothing can keep you from me, and nothing can keep me from you (vv. 31–32, 35–39).

When you say forgiveness, this is what you mean. I thank you and praise you—my Father, Grace Giver, and Friend!

Amen.

With Jesus in the Wilderness

Matthew 4:1–11

This petition from the sixth path pairs well with the brief account in Matthew 4 of Jesus' temptation in the desert. There, after Jesus had been weakened from a lengthy fast, the devil tried to entice him to turn stones into bread, leap from a tower, and worship a false god.

Classic interpretations group the story into three types of temptations that we all face: to satisfy our physical desires (lust); to show off our abilities (pride); and to get and keep control (power). Think through the urges you have—both little and large—that can get you in trouble. Put it in bodily terms: What does your stomach want? What does your heart want? What does your head want? In all three areas, we can choose to follow Jesus, or we can choose counterfeit goods and false gods that lead us astray.

The more you sit with this compact story, the more you'll find yourself in it, and the more you'll discover ways to pray through this scripture.

⁜

1   Then Jesus was led up by the Spirit into the wilderness to be tempted by the devil. 2 He fasted forty days and forty nights, and afterwards he was famished. 3 The tempter came and said to him, "If you are the Son of God, command these stones to become loaves of bread." 4 But he answered, "It is written,

> 'One does not live by bread alone,
> but by every word that comes from the mouth of God.'"

5   Then the devil took him to the holy city and placed him on the pinnacle of the temple, 6 saying to him, "If you are the Son of God, throw yourself down; for it is written,

> 'He will command his angels concerning you,'
> and 'On their hands they will bear you up,
> so that you will not dash your foot against a stone.'"

7   Jesus said to him, "Again it is written,

> 'Do not put the Lord your God to the test.'"

8   Again, the devil took him to a very high mountain and showed him all the kingdoms of the world and their splendor; 9 and he said to him, "All these I will give you, if you will fall down and worship me." 10 Jesus said to him, "Away with you, Satan! for it is written,

'Worship the Lord your God,
and serve only him.'"

11 Then the devil left him, and suddenly angels came and
waited on him.

Lord Jesus,

You were led to a lonely place, where temptation found you (v. 1). When I am tempted, help me to remember that you have been there, too.

✦

The tempter offered you food, but it was not the nourishment you needed (vv. 3–4). Where do I take shortcuts? Where do I fulfill my desires with an immediate payoff instead of what is lasting? Show me, kind Spirit.

✦

You were tempted to show off your power, but you resisted (vv. 5–7). Where do I hold tightly to reputation and pride? Where do I insist on winning? Make me aware of the places where ego rules my heart and mind.

✦

Immediate power could have been yours, but you chose a humble way (vv. 8–10). Where am I grasping for power or control? Where do I want authority that is not mine? Show me your way of finding strength in weakness, Jesus.

✦

Help me in my daily struggle against temptation. May your angels guard my way, and may your Spirit set me free—for your glory and my well-being (v. 11).

Amen.

Parables of Plenty and Want

Luke 18:1–25

Jesus told many parables illustrating this Beatitude, including these four stories in Luke. All of them explore different sorts of spiritual, social, and material poverty. Taken together, they show that God accepts those who come to him humbly, and resists those who are haughty and proud.

We meet a widow who persists in seeking justice from a corrupt judge, even though she is practically powerless to get a fair hearing. We meet a tax collector (despised by religious types of the day) who knows he needs God and doesn't mind showing it. We meet young children whose innocence makes them already fit for the kingdom. And we meet a rich man whose worldly possessions and power obscure his deep need.

Read the stories attentively, treating them like poems or koans that invite contemplation and reward patience. You might even memorize one, then call it to mind throughout your day.

2 "In a certain city there was a judge who neither feared God nor had respect for people. **3** In that city there was a widow who kept coming to him and saying, 'Grant me justice against my opponent.' **4** For a while he refused; but later he said to himself, 'Though I have no fear of God and no respect for anyone, **5** yet because this widow keeps bothering me, I will grant her justice, so that she may not wear me out by continually coming.'" **6** And the Lord said, "Listen to what the unjust judge says. **7** And will not God grant justice to his chosen ones who cry to him day and night?" . . .

10 "Two men went up to the temple to pray, one a Pharisee and the other a tax collector. **11** The Pharisee, standing by himself, was praying thus, 'God, I thank you that I am not like other people: thieves, rogues, adulterers, or even like this tax collector. **12** I fast twice a week; I give a tenth of all my income.' **13** But the tax collector, standing far off, would not even look up to heaven, but was beating his breast and saying, 'God, be merciful to me, a sinner!' **14** I tell you, this man went down to his home justified rather than the other; for all who exalt themselves will be humbled, but all who humble themselves will be exalted." . . .

16 "Let the little children come to me, and do not stop them; for it is to such as these that the kingdom of God belongs. **17** . . . Whoever does not receive the kingdom of God as a little child will never enter it." . . .

22　　Jesus said to him, ". . . Sell all that you own and distribute the money to the poor, and you will have treasure in heaven; then come, follow me." 23 But when he heard this, he became sad; for he was very rich. 24 Jesus looked at him and said, "How hard it is for those who have wealth to enter the kingdom of God!"

Lord Jesus,

I want to be like the widow who keeps pleading for justice in the face of oppression. Help me not to give up. Sometimes I rationalize that I'm not positioned to accomplish enough for the weak and the disadvantaged. But that's not true (vv. 2–7).

I want to be like the tax collector, who won't let his awareness of his sins keep him from casting himself on your mercies. I can be as self-conscious and proud as a Pharisee, but it's the tax collector's humility I ask for today (vv. 10–14).

I want to be like the children who came so easily to you. I can be too grown-up for my own good. Help me shed my know-it-all, "been there, done that" ways (vv. 16–17).

And like a person of wealth and power, I want meaning in life without giving up what I already have to get it. Help me let go. Change my heart, Lord (vv. 22–24).

You said your kingdom belongs to the poor in spirit. Where is the kingdom ready to break through in my life, if I'll just persist, get honest about my real need, get off my high horse, put down my status and stuff? Show me.

Thank you that your gospel is for someone exactly like me.

Amen.

Manna from Heaven

Exodus 16:2–16

When Jesus told his disciples to ask for their daily bread, he may have been alluding to a well-known story of God's provision. In Exodus, Moses leads the Israelites in an en masse escape from Egypt, where they have been enslaved by Pharaoh for centuries. But not long after their escape, they begin to worry about how they'll survive on their own. They complain to Moses that in Egypt, at least, they had plenty of food, but "you have brought us out into this wilderness to kill this whole assembly with hunger" (Exodus 16:3). Moses is frustrated with their grumbling, but God responds simply and miraculously: each day, manna arrives like the morning dew.

This chapter provides rich material for prayer. Besides the wonderful story of bread from heaven, we find illustrations of many common human foibles: for example, our tendencies to complain, to idealize the past, to mistreat leaders, and to chafe against even commonsense rules. We also recognize our persistent doubts that the God who provided our bread today will provide again tomorrow.

Fortunately, over and around all the evidence of human weakness and doubt, we see our Father's commitment to our well-being.

2 The whole congregation of the Israelites complained against Moses and Aaron in the wilderness. **3** The Israelites said to them, "If only we had died by the hand of the Lord in the land of Egypt, when we sat by the fleshpots and ate our fill of bread; for you have brought us out into this wilderness to kill this whole assembly with hunger."

4 Then the Lord said to Moses, "I am going to rain bread from heaven for you, and each day the people shall go out and gather enough for that day. In that way I will test them, whether they will follow my instruction or not. **5** On the sixth day, when they prepare what they bring in, it will be twice as much as they gather on other days." **6** So Moses and Aaron said to all the Israelites, "In the evening you shall know that it was the Lord who brought you out of the land of Egypt, **7** and in the morning you shall see the glory of the Lord, because he has heard your complaining against the Lord." . . . **11** The Lord spoke to Moses and said, **12** "I have heard the complaining of the Israelites; say to them, 'At twilight you shall eat meat, and in the morning you shall have your fill of bread; then you shall know that I am the Lord your God.'"

13 In the evening quails came up and covered the camp; and in the morning there was a layer of dew around the camp. **14** When the layer of dew lifted, there on the surface of the wilderness was a fine flaky substance, as fine as frost on the ground. **15** When the Israelites saw it, they said to one another, "What is it?" For they did not know what it was. Moses said to them, "It is the bread that the Lord has given you to eat. **16** This is what the Lord has commanded: 'Gather as much of it as each of you needs, an omer to a person according to the number of persons, all providing for those in their own tents.'"

My Provider,

Where am I lost in a wilderness of need, want, or sin? Show me, Lord. I want to be found by you.

◆

What about my past might I be idealizing, or wasting time and energy longing for? Help me see the illusions that are robbing me of today (v. 3).

◆

Am I prone to complain, even when you are providing for me? Please show me how and when (vv. 6–7).

◆

You provide so generously for my wants and needs (vv. 11–12). But some situations consistently trigger my doubts about your provision in the future. Show them to me. And, where does your generosity trigger my greed instead of greater charity with others? Please, gracious Provider, help me see the truth (vv. 13–16).

◆

Loving Provider, let this be the measure of my trust in you: that what I want is what you want for me. Thank you that you are with me on my journey. Help me to receive your gifts, put them to good use, and rest—no matter what—in your unfailing goodness.

Amen.

God Speaks from the Whirlwind

Job 38

The Bible is replete with passages that illuminate what it means to fear God. But it's hard to beat Job 38, in which an explanation is given by no less an authority than God.

For thirty-seven chapters, we've seen Job's previously favored existence reduced to ruin, and listened to his understandable litany of complaints. Job's personal tragedy sets up the driving question of the book, a question that his three friends famously try to answer, and one that has haunted generations of sufferers since: "Why do bad things happen to good people?"

In chapter 38, God answers with questions of his own: Who are you to question me? Don't you realize I'm the creator of everything, the all-powerful and all-knowing God? God then proceeds to describe his utter pleasure in everything he has made and done—from setting the universe into motion, to caring for even the most unusual creatures of earth, to foiling specific plans of the enemies of God's people.

The main takeaway for Job? Job is a human, and is not God. Only God is God.

Read these selections from Job 38, preparing yourself to pray and receive this gift—what the wheel calls the fear of the Lord—as an understanding that gives God his due. As the old hymn title declares, "This Is My Father's World."

*

1   Then the Lord answered Job out of the whirlwind. . . .
3   "Gird up your loins like a man,
          I will question you, and you shall declare to me.

4   "Where were you when I laid the foundation of the earth?
          Tell me, if you have understanding.
5   Who determined its measurements—surely you know!
          Or who stretched the line upon it?
6   On what were its bases sunk,
          or who laid its cornerstone
7   when the morning stars sang together
          and all the heavenly beings shouted for joy?

8   "Or who shut in the sea with doors
          when it burst out from the womb?—
9   when I made the clouds its garment,
          and thick darkness its swaddling band,
10   and prescribed bounds for it,
          and set bars and doors,
11   and said, 'Thus far shall you come, and no farther,
          and here shall your proud waves be stopped'?

12   "Have you commanded the morning since your days began,
          and caused the dawn to know its place,
13   so that it might take hold of the skirts of the earth,
          and the wicked be shaken out of it? . . .

34   "Can you lift up your voice to the clouds,
        so that a flood of waters may cover you?

35   Can you send forth lightnings, so that they may go
        and say to you, 'Here we are'?

36   Who has put wisdom in the inward parts,
        or given understanding to the mind?"

Almighty God,

You are God. I am not. But I forget. I behave as if I am God. I attempt to take control of things. I assume I'm in charge, that freedom to act means I hold the keys to my own life.

When things go wrong, I wonder why bad things happen. But you remind me that you are God. And I am not (vv. 4–7).

You are the creator of the universe. You put all life and matter into motion, including me (vv. 8–11). My drive to create, to build, to manage reflects your nature in me, but I am not you.

You are the center of all things—inside atoms, down to the quarks, you are there, holding it all together. Sometimes I make my happiness a reason to trust you, and my pain a reason to doubt you. But you are beyond my happiness and my pain.

You are the reason for everything. And I am not. Every bird, every blade of grass, everything that swims in the ocean, every cloud and star—it's all a glimpse of you (vv. 34–36).

You are too wonderful for my mind to grasp. I can hardly imagine you. But I want to live in awe of you today—on my face in worship and love before you.

Help me to know and see you more truly, and hold you in reverence no matter what happens. Because you are good, and only you are God.

Amen.

The Stranger Who Stopped to Help

Luke 10:25–37

Your prayers related to the "mercy" Beatitude in the wheel will be challenged by the story Jesus tells in this passage. Even if you're familiar with the story, it's worth looking at again with new eyes, because it's extraordinary.

A lawyer asks Jesus for a definition of the term "neighbor," because he's trying to understand—or, rather, get around—what the scriptures mean when they say, "Love your neighbor as yourself." In response, Jesus tells the story of a Jewish man who is robbed and left for dead on the side of the road. One after the other, two upstanding citizens walk right by, ignoring him. Then a despised Samaritan comes along, doctors up the wounded man, finds lodging for him, and foots the entire bill.

Imagine this story being told today and substitute the term "Muslim" for "Samaritan," and you'll have a pretty good sense of the effect Jesus was trying to create.

But the merciful person's identity is only part of the point; the other part is his action—he saw someone in need and stopped everything to care for him, sacrificing his time and money for a stranger.

As you think through this story, you'll see how Jesus is calling for us to be extravagant in handing out mercy. Whoever needs help, whatever community has need is our neighbor. They belong to us, and our mercy belongs to them.

*

25 Just then a lawyer stood up to test Jesus. "Teacher," he said, "what must I do to inherit eternal life?"

26 He said to him, "What is written in the law? What do you read there?"

27 He answered, "You shall love the Lord your God with all your heart, and with all your soul, and with all your strength, and with all your mind; and your neighbor as yourself."

28 And he said to him, "You have given the right answer; do this, and you will live."

29 But wanting to justify himself, he asked Jesus, "And who is my neighbor?"

30 Jesus replied, "A man was going down from Jerusalem to Jericho, and fell into the hands of robbers, who stripped him, beat him, and went away, leaving him half dead.

31 Now by chance a priest was going down that road; and when he saw him, he passed by on the other side.

32 So likewise a Levite, when he came to the place and saw him, passed by on the other side.

33 But a Samaritan while traveling came near him; and when he saw him, he was moved with pity.

34 He went to him and bandaged his wounds, having poured oil and wine on them. Then he put him on his own animal, brought him to an inn, and took care of him.

35 The next day he took out two denarii, gave them to the

innkeeper, and said, 'Take care of him; and when I come back, I will repay you whatever more you spend.'

36 Which of these three, do you think, was a neighbor to the man who fell into the hands of the robbers?"

37 He said, "The one who showed him mercy." Jesus said to him, "Go and do likewise."

Lord,

I'm supposed to spread mercy like confetti at a parade, because that's what love demands, and I want to love you with all my heart, mind, and strength (v. 27).

Sometimes in my own hurry or self-absorption I'm apt to rush by someone in a crisis, someone who needs my help (vv. 31–32).

But help me to pause and see those who need compassionate attention:
    ~Those who require sacrifice from me, who could cost me time, effort, or money (vv. 34–35)
    ~Those to whom I don't feel obligated
    ~Those, even friends and family, who have wronged me
    ~Those who ignore me, or who are too busy for me, or who have neglected me
    ~Those who struggle in proximity to me but whom I've learned to barely notice
    ~Those you have placed in my conscience by the nudging of your Spirit
These are the ones you want me to call "neighbor." Help me to have mercy on and take responsibility for my neighborhood (vv. 36–37).

May your mercies grow in me as I become more and more skilled at sharing with others your extravagant grace. Free me from judgment, and fill me with love.

Amen.

PART 4

The Bands of the Wheel

I n ordering the parts of this book, we assumed most readers would be eager to dive into actually praying with the wheel, so we limited the amount of background material we presented to begin with. In this part, we provide more information about the wheel's four primary texts: the Lord's Prayer (Our Father), Gifts of the Holy Spirit, Events in the Life of Christ, and the Beatitudes.

❋ THE SEVEN PETITIONS OF THE LORD'S PRAYER

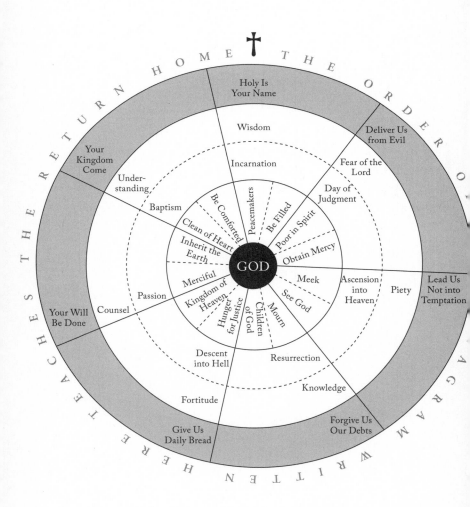

THE RETURN HOME · THE ORDER OF A GRAM WRITTEN HERE TEACHES

Holy Is Your Name

Deliver Us from Evil

Your Kingdom Come

Lead Us Not into Temptation

Your Will Be Done

Give Us Daily Bread

Forgive Us Our Debts

Wisdom
Incarnation
Understanding
Baptism
Passion
Counsel
Descent into Hell
Fortitude

Fear of the Lord
Day of Judgment
Ascension into Heaven
Piety
Resurrection
Knowledge

Be Comforted
Peacemakers
Be Filled
Poor in Spirit
Clean of Heart
Inherit the Earth
Obtain Mercy
Merciful
Meek
Kingdom of Heaven
Hunger for Justice
Children of God
Mourn
See God

GOD

When Jesus guides his disciples in how to pray, he is not simply instructing; he's heeding a request. And the Father, he indicates, will do likewise, since petitions are the backbone of the Lord's Prayer.

This short prayer has been a foundation of Christian life since the beginning. In the Didache, a manual for churches dating from around the second century, believers were instructed to say the Lord's Prayer three times a day. Centuries later, Augustine proposed that just reciting this prayer could prompt the forgiving of smaller sins.

The classic reading of the Lord's Prayer holds that the first three petitions deal with how we relate to God and the divine, and the last four deal mostly with life on earth. The two are actually more closely connected than you might think, though, because elsewhere in the gospels Jesus makes it clear that the kingdom of God is already here, within each one of us. That means that when we pray *your kingdom come,* we're not asking for Jesus to glide down from heaven in a chariot and escort us home. We're asking that God's sovereignty be honored and actualized more and more in our world, and in our hearts. And when we pray *your will be done,* we accept that God can see the bigger picture that now eludes us. *Your will be done* is a test of our willingness to right-size ourselves and our wishes.

The ending of the third petition, *on earth as it is in heaven,* signals a shift in the prayer. So far, the petitions have all had to do directly with God: his name, his kingdom, and his purposes. From here to the end of the prayer, the primary focus will be on more human matters. Each petition is an expression of faith in God, or an invitation for us to reach for faith even if we don't feel it.

For example, the fourth petition expresses our dependence on the Father's provision and care. We need daily bread. The "daily" part here is significant, because it speaks to our level of trust. It's not enough just to rely on God for today but to expect that, by tomorrow, we'll be able to take care of ourselves. God is our daily provider, who welcomes us into a lifelong relationship of trust.

We are also dependent on others, as the fifth petition—*forgive us our debts*—makes clear. Thomas Aquinas says this is the only petition in the Lord's Prayer that is conditional: we must be willing to forgive our neighbor before God will forgive us (Luke 6:37). But, as we all know, forgiveness doesn't come easily, especially when the hurt goes deep.

It is interesting that the fifth petition—*forgive us our debts, as we forgive our debtors*—leads immediately into the sixth one, which asks God not to let us fall into sin. One of the ways God achieves this is by giving us the grace to realize that the plank in our own eye dwarfs the speck in our neighbor's. This is also a foundation of forgiveness.

The seventh petition asks the Father to safeguard us from evil. Augustine says that "evil" here includes illness, sin, and afflictions. But to have God deliver us from evil is not the same as to have God make evil disappear. Just as the other petitions asked us to trust in the Father's judgment, this one demands that we put our faith in him. He will comfort us in our suffering and give us strength to bear whatever is coming. That is deliverance enough.

These last four petitions invite us to practice God's holiness—trusting in God's provision, forgiving others, and resisting temptation and evil—so that we can live out the petitions of the prayer's first half. It's like we're being told that if we're serious about helping God's name become holy, his kingdom to come, and his will to be done, we must be intentional about taking up our part.

As a final thought, note that the Lord's Prayer always uses the language of "we"; the prayer is in the first-person plural, not the first-person singular. The petitions Christ taught us are intended for the entire community of the faithful, not just one person. It's the "Our Father," not the "My Father." Whether we pray this in a group or alone, Jesus' prayer affirms that we are members of a living community.

⚜ GIFTS OF THE HOLY SPIRIT

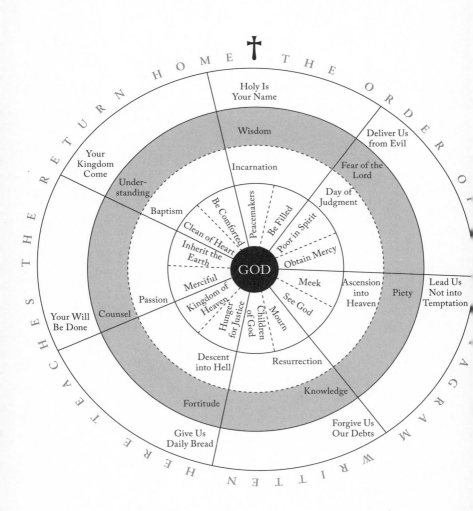

Outer ring: THE RETURN HOME · THE ORDER OF · DIAGRAM WRITTEN HERE TEACHES · THE RETURN

Cross symbol (top)

Petitions (outer labeled ring):
- Holy Is Your Name
- Deliver Us from Evil
- Lead Us Not into Temptation
- Forgive Us Our Debts
- Give Us Daily Bread
- Your Will Be Done
- Your Kingdom Come

Gifts (shaded ring):
- Wisdom
- Fear of the Lord
- Piety
- Knowledge
- Fortitude
- Counsel
- Understanding

Middle ring:
- Incarnation
- Day of Judgment
- Ascension into Heaven
- Resurrection
- Descent into Hell
- Passion
- Baptism

Inner ring (Beatitudes virtues):
- Peacemakers
- Be Filled
- Poor in Spirit
- Obtain Mercy
- Meek
- See God
- Mourn
- Children of God
- Hunger for Justice
- Kingdom of Heaven
- Merciful
- Inherit the Earth
- Clean of Heart
- Be Comforted

Center: GOD

Many Christians associate the phrase "gifts of the spirit" with the letters of Paul, where he lists spiritual gifts at work in the Church (see 1 Corinthians 12 and Romans 12). But the Prayer Wheel's gifts of the spirit come from a passage in the Book of Isaiah. In a prophecy that came to be understood by Christians as a direct reference to Jesus, Isaiah lists seven spirits that would accompany the Messiah on earth: wisdom, understanding, counsel, fortitude, knowledge, piety, and the fear of the Lord. (The gift of "piety" does not actually appear in the passage, but "fear of the Lord" appears twice, and tradition translates the first instance as piety.)

The early Church read these "spirits" as gifts of the Holy Spirit, and included them in the baptismal rite, praying that each gift would accompany the new Christian. To this day, the Roman Catholic Church uses Isaiah 11:2–3 in prayers at a believer's confirmation. Anglican and Lutheran churches also make use of these gifts and for the same reasons: They are given to all believers in order to help us become like Christ. They are a support system. They are God saying: "You want to live well? Here, these gifts will help."

Wisdom, in classic Christian teaching, helps us desire the things of God in the sense that our very being conforms to his ways and his will—from the inside out, we think, feel, and live according to the ways of the Lord. Wisdom has less to do with what you believe or know to be true, and more to do with what you feel, want, and love. Wisdom drives you from within. When you love the ways of God and live according to that love, you are living in wisdom.

Understanding describes a comprehension of spiritual things. This gift is essential because spirituality can be confusing. Consider Jesus' parables, and how often the disciples and religious leaders were baffled by what he was saying. Spiritual truths are not as easily provable as 2 + 2 = 4. Comprehending them requires patience as well as trial and error. The spiritual gift of understanding helps us to grow into these insights over time, kneading them into our lives like yeast into dough.

Counsel is right judgment, the ability to follow the Holy Spirit's leading and choose right from wrong. Think of wisdom and understanding as providing continual grounding for your life, and counsel as providing more targeted direction. Counsel is closely associated in scripture with the Holy Spirit, also known as the *Counselor*—that "still, small voice" that is trying to help us discern the path ahead.

Fortitude describes a combination of strength and courage founded on the knowledge that you can rely on God's power. In the wheel, it's associated with Christ's "descent into hell" and the "hunger for justice," because doing justice involves contending with evil. Fortitude is living by your convictions, standing up for truth, and championing the innocent and weak in the face of powerful opposition.

Knowledge has to do not just with *what* to know but with *how* to know it. It's the ability to grasp God's truth—as a set of ideas and facts, yes, but also as a way of understanding those ideas and facts. The Prayer Wheel, in keeping with ancient Church tradition, pairs the spiritual gift of knowledge with the resurrection: the resurrection of Jesus is, according to Church doctrine, a knowable fact. It actually happened on a certain day at a certain time. But it also involves what we might call "spiritual knowing." When Paul writes, "I want to know Christ and the power of his resurrection and the sharing of his sufferings by becoming like him in his death, if somehow I may attain the resurrection from the dead" (Philippians 3:10), he's suggesting that we know the resurrection in a process of "becoming like" Christ. Not just by studying with his mind but by *becoming* with his life.

Piety describes a reverence for God that expresses itself in holy living. Note that the wheel puts "piety" directly in line with "meek." Pious people exhibit meekness, which is gentleness, purity, patience—the opposite of violence, of taking advantage or being overbearing. The gift of piety leads toward a simple, uncompromising devotion to God.

Fear of the Lord, we're told several times in the Bible, "is the beginning of wisdom." The fear of the Lord is not fright, exactly; it's an acknowledgment that God is mighty, and that in comparison to him, we are not. The fear of the Lord is a gift because it puts us in our right place in relationship to an all-powerful God who makes plain what living in deference to his will looks like.

⚜ EVENTS IN THE LIFE OF CHRIST

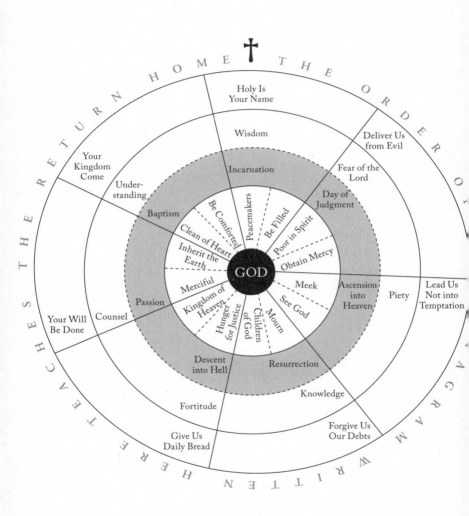

The list of seven events in the life of Jesus Christ is the wheel's special bonus text. The Lord's Prayer, gifts of the Holy Spirit, and the Beatitudes are all quotations from scripture. The events are not. The other three texts had been grouped together and compared since the fifth century; the events were added to this group much later, and their addition was a kind of breakthrough.

When Augustine gathered the first three texts, he had a relatively modest goal: to illuminate the Lord's Prayer with two passages of almost equal importance, the gifts and the Beatitudes. No text *about* Christ was necessary for this. After all, Christ was already present in his words, and everyone knew the background story.

But in the mid-800s, Paschasius Radbertus added what he called the *septem bona,* or the "Seven Good Things"—Christ's life, from incarnation to the last judgment. Radbertus probably thought that the list (incarnation, baptism, passion, descent into hell, resurrection, ascension into heaven, and the Day of Judgment) paired perfectly with the list of the Spirit's gifts from Isaiah 11—which was, after all, a prophecy of Christ's life. The seven events came readily to hand: all but baptism were included in the Apostles' Creed, one of the Church's foundational statements of belief.

Intentionally or unintentionally, adding the events transformed the wheel. The Christian story is more than just a set of theological ideas. It is the narrative of a person who was born of the Virgin Mary, suffered and died, rose on the third day, and will come again.

With these snapshots from the gospels added, the combined texts could express doctrines of the faith that had previously been beyond the reach of the wheel. Here's one example: the Trinity. Suddenly there was a text explicitly identified with the Father (the Lord's Prayer), a text for the Holy Spirit (the gifts), and a text for the Son (the events). All were encompassed in this four-part pocket review of the faith, and all were now ready for the wheel maker to invite them into a circle of relationship.

⚜ THE BEATITUDES

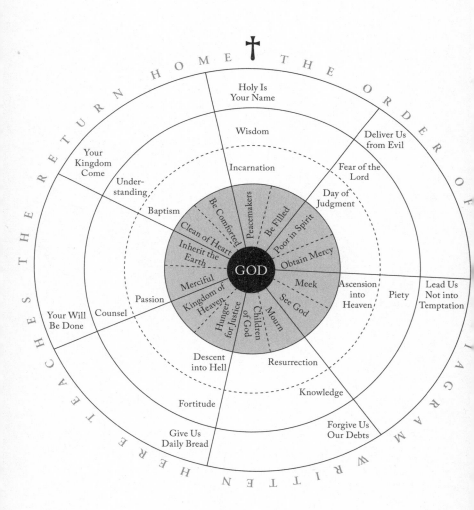

THE RETURN HOME — THE ORDER OF DIAGRAM WRITTEN HERE TEACHES

Holy Is Your Name

Wisdom

Incarnation

Your Kingdom Come

Understanding

Baptism

Deliver Us from Evil

Fear of the Lord

Day of Judgment

Peacemakers

Be Comforted

Be Filled

Clean of Heart

Poor in Spirit

Inherit the Earth

Obtain Mercy

GOD

Merciful

Meek

Kingdom of Heaven

See God

Ascension into Heaven

Piety

Hunger for Justice

Mourn

Children of God

Passion

Counsel

Your Will Be Done

Descent into Hell

Resurrection

Lead Us Not into Temptation

Fortitude

Knowledge

Give Us Daily Bread

Forgive Us Our Debts

The Beatitudes of Jesus have found their way into songs and sermons for two thousand years. In fact, they've become so familiar that Christians sometimes skip lightly through them, as we might a nursery rhyme.

That approach is too simple, because there's an apparent paradox in each verse. The person being described as "blessed" or "happy" in each is poor, grieving, persecuted, or hungry. In N. T. Wright's translation of the New Testament, he captures both the joy and the unlikely nature of the pairings:

> Wonderful news for the poor in spirit! The kingdom of heaven is yours.
> Wonderful news for the mourners! You're going to be comforted.
> Wonderful news for the meek! You're going to inherit the earth. . . .

When read with care, these promises require a great deal of us. The Beatitudes ask us to believe that unlucky people in unenviable situations are actually blessed. No one willingly signs up for pain, sadness, or other people's ridicule. Yet here Jesus suggests that the more we experience those things, the more God is with us.

It's precisely because the Beatitudes reach into some of the darker regions of life that we need to pray them. They teach us that, in the end, there's no darkness or pain God won't redeem. Richard Foster wrote that the Beatitudes are a kind of "Jubilee inversion," in which Jesus took all the people and situations that were thought to be "unblessed and unblessable" and showed instead that "in the forgiving, receiving, accepting life of God's kingdom they too are blessed."

So there's a big difference between hearing the Beatitudes passively in church and praying them actively, introducing ourselves and all of our pain into the act. By doing so, we are inviting God into the deepest conflicts and disappointments of life, and asking him to bless the very things we most wish didn't exist.

Perhaps this is why the wheel locates the Beatitudes closest to home, to the heart of God. In praying them, we are asking God to walk with us through the pain and come out on the other side, where we can be better equipped to do his work, and where he promises there is always blessing.

NEXT STEPS

We began this book with a quotation from Jeremiah: "Stand at the crossroads, and look, and ask for the ancient paths, where the good way lies; and walk in it, and find rest for your souls" (6:16). We've seen that the Prayer Wheel is one such proven path, forged in a time very different from ours, yet speaking to the same questions and uncertainties believers face today: How can I know God's will? Where do I fit into the kingdom? And how can I grow closer to God?

We hope that this introduction to a lost spiritual practice has refreshed your faith and brought to your conversations with God a new range and depth. We also hope that by now you are comfortable enough with the basic architecture and content of the Prayer Wheel that you will want to experiment with it and make it your own. Like earnest pilgrims of earlier times, you can take the tools and traditions, and bring your own reflection and creativity to bear.

Consider creating a diagram of the Prayer Wheel in which the individual rings spin independently, so that every time you "spin the wheel" you come up with a different prayer combination. You might want to tell your friends about what the wheel is teaching you, and then pray it together. Or you could simply start back at the beginning of this book and do the seven weeks of prayer again, this time with additional clarity as the individual pieces click into place and the wheel makes sense as a unit.

Whatever your approach, we're confident that as you pray the wheel you'll find fresh insights and renewed faith. The Prayer Wheel has many paths, but all of them lead home.

NOTES

Introduction

The abbot's high praise for theological diagrams is found in Jeffrey F. Hamburger, "Haec Figura Demonstrat: Diagrams in an Early Thirteenth-Century Parisian Copy of Lothar de Segni's *De Missarum Mysteriis*," *Wiener Jahrbuch für Kunstgeschichte* 58 (2009), 8.

Mother Teresa's quote about prayer is from *No Greater Love* (Novato, CA: New World Library, 1997), 14.

The "God alone could teach us" excerpt is from Tertullian, as quoted in Roy Hammerling, *The Lord's Prayer in the Early Church: The Pearl of Great Price* (New York: Palgrave Macmillan, 2010), 6.

The Peter Chrysologus statement about the angels standing in awe of prayer is from Hammerling's book (4).

The description of Ramon Llull's over-the-top wheel construction is from Michael W. Evans, "The Geometry of the Mind," *Architectural Association Quarterly* 12, no. 4 (1980), 32–55.

Part 1

Week 1, "Connecting This Path with the Next": At first glance, there's considerable overlap among the gifts of wisdom, understanding, counsel, and knowledge. One of the best resources to help you distinguish among them is Thomas Keating, *Fruits and Gifts of the Holy Spirit* (Snowmass, CO: Lantern Books, 2000).

Week 7, Day 5: The different Greek words for "poor" are explained in William Barclay, *The Beatitudes and the Lord's Prayer for Everyman* (New York: Harper & Row, 1963), 20–22. Barclay notes that the difference between *penes* and *ptochos* is "between the man who is poor and frugal and the man who is destitute and a beggar."

Part 2

To express gratitude: For more on Jesus' feeding of the five thousand in John and the scene's connection to the Passover, see N. T. Wright, *John for Everyone, Part I: Chapters 1–10* (London: SPCK, 2002), 71–73.

Part 4

Augustine's ideas about the Lord's Prayer can be found in Thomas Aquinas, *The Three Greatest Prayers: Commentaries on the Lord's Prayer, the Hail Mary, and the Apostles' Creed* (Manchester, NH: Sophia Institute Press, 1990), 102.

In the gifts of the Holy Spirit, the original Hebrew text from Isaiah 11 has only six enumerated gifts. Piety is missing, and "fear of the Lord" appears twice. When the Old Testament was translated into Greek in the second century BCE, the translators chose to render the first mention of "fear of the Lord" as "piety," bringing the number of gifts to seven. See Mitch Finley, *The Seven Gifts of the Holy Spirit* (Liguori, MO: Liguori Publications, 2001), xi.

Paschasius Radbertus's formulation of the "Seven Good Things" is described briefly in Ulrich Rehm's book *Bebilderte Vaterunser-Erklärungen des Mittelalters* (Baden-Baden, Germany: Valentin Koerner, 1994), 55.

For N. T. Wright's rendition of the Beatitudes as "wonderful news!" see *Matthew for Everyone, Part I: Chapters 1–15* (London: SPCK, 2002), 34.

Richard Foster's notion of the Beatitudes as a kind of "Jubilee inversion" is found in his book *Streams of Living Water: Celebrating the Great Tradition of Christian Faith* (San Francisco: HarperSanFrancisco, 1998), 12.

For readers interested in the composition of this particular book: It was David Van Biema who first encountered the Liesborn Prayer Wheel and conceived the idea for a book. In the writing he worked almost exclusively on the explanatory and history sections. All three authors collaborated to define the concept for the book, with further aid from the publisher. Jana Riess and Patton Dodd wrote the prayers that make up the majority of the content.

ACKNOWLEDGMENTS

The authors would like to thank Sandra Hindman and Les Enluminures for first alerting David to the existence of the Liesborn Gospels book (via the invaluable A. Larry Ross) and the hidden treasure it harbored inside: the Prayer Wheel. In particular, we're grateful to Sandra for allowing us to use the Latin image of the wheel so readers can see it in its original beauty. We also thank illustrator Darrel Frost for his elegant modern renderings of the wheel, streamlining it for devotional use today. Those renderings informed the designer's illustrations in this book.

We consulted many experts in the fields of medieval history, religion, and art. We are especially grateful to Dr. Lauren Mancia, whose early enthusiasm and continuing expertise were crucial to us. Dr. Ulrich Rehm, whose dissertation is one of the only full-length treatments of medieval prayer wheels, pointed us in helpful directions. Dr. Roy Hammerling aided us both through his book on the Lord's Prayer and with his generous advice and support. Roy in turn brought in several of his colleagues who were of aid. Father James Martin helped us understand the wheel's potential for believers today, and Brian Finnerty offered vital observations. Dr. Jeffrey Hamburger helped us understand the importance of geometric figures and the wheel's development through history. Clark Strand saw the wheel differently. Laurence Bond was our superb research assistant. John Lyon, Julie Murray, and Tiffany Vann Sprecher also assisted us in various phases of research.

Early readers, wheel users, and friends provided valuable feedback, in particular Robyn Gibboney, Rob Weinert-Kendt, Nancy

Hopkins-Greene, Ansley Roan, Daniel Grothe, Matt Burnett, Dawn Clement, Marcus Goodyear, Paul Soupiset, Dan Roloff, Barbara Herzfeld, Yonat Shimron, and the Reverends Ann Kansfield and Jennifer Aull and their congregation at Greenpoint Church in Brooklyn. Regular visitors to the wheel's Facebook page caught our enthusiasm for the wheel and contributed their own ideas. We're particularly grateful to Mary Askren, who emerged as a thoughtful commenter and took over the page for a time when the three of us were busy writing this book.

No book is created in isolation, and this one would not have been possible without the shepherding and early championing of David's literary agent, Todd Shuster of Aevitas Creative Management. Todd helped us find a wonderful home for the project with Convergent at Penguin Random House. We are especially grateful to our editors, David Kopp and Derek Reed, for their passion and careful shaping of this manuscript, and to designer Elizabeth Rendfleisch, for making the wheel both beautiful and accessible.

In addition, some personal thanks from each of us:

Patton would like to thank his coauthors—David for proposing this project, Jana for being game, and both of them for being so smart, capable, and good-spirited. Thanks to Father Matt for enthusiastic and instructive initial feedback, and to Todd Skinner for helping keep things on track. Thanks to Tara Owens and Alice Rhee for deep and daily counsel. Above all, thanks to Michaela, Bel, Henry, and Lou, the greatest gifts I'll ever know.

Jana would like to thank David and Patton for their creativity and diligence; the Adult Forum at the Episcopal Church of the Redeemer in Cincinnati for early feedback; her writing group for ideas and inspiration; and the Mercantile Library in Cincinnati for providing a warm and hospitable "third place" in which to write. Most of all, she is grateful to her husband for his enthusiasm and well of patience. She dedicates this labor of love to her friend and former colleague Phyllis Tickle, who died in 2015, when we were just dreaming up the book. May she rest in peace and rise in glory.

David thanks his coauthors; Julian, Allison, Mick, Sharon, Morris; and all those whose ears he bent.

ABOUT THE AUTHORS

PATTON DODD is a writer and editor whose work has appeared in the *Wall Street Journal*, the *Washington Post*, TheAtlantic.com, CNN.com, the *Financial Times, Newsweek, Slate, Christianity Today, Shambhala Sun*, and more. He has also appeared on a range of television and radio shows, including *Hannity* and the *Laura Ingraham Show* as well as on ESPN Radio and National Public Radio. He has served as editor of several of the largest religion news and commentary websites, including Beliefnet, Patheos, and OnFaith. Patton is the editor or coeditor of several books, including a memoir, *My Faith So Far: A Story of Conversion and Confusion*. He holds a PhD in religious studies from Boston University.

JANA RIESS holds degrees in religion from Wellesley College, Princeton Theological Seminary, and Columbia University. She is a senior columnist for Religion News Service and speaks often to the media about issues pertaining to religion in America. She is the author, coauthor, or editor of many books, including *Flunking Sainthood: A Year of Breaking the Sabbath, Forgetting to Pray, and Still Loving My Neighbor*, named one of the top ten religion books of the year by *Publishers Weekly* in 2011.

DAVID VAN BIEMA was head religion writer at *Time* from 1999 to 2009. He wrote twenty-five cover stories for the magazine, as well as covers for *Life* magazine, *People*, and the *Washington Post Magazine*. His recent work has appeared in *Time*, the *Washington Post*, TheAtlantic.com, the Religion News Service, and other venues.

He has won numerous religion newswriting prizes. His interviewees have included the Dalai Lama, the Archbishop of Canterbury (Rowan Williams at the time), Rick Warren, and Thich Nhat Hanh. He is the author of the book *Mother Teresa: The Life and Works of a Modern Saint*.